BECOMING MORE
THAN A GOOD BIBLE STUDY GIRL

OTHER BOOKS BY LYSA TERKEURST

BECOMING MORE
THAN A GOOD BIBLE STUDY GIRL

LYSA TERKEURST

ZONDERVAN®

ZONDERVAN.com/
AUTHORTRACKER
follow your favorite authors

ZONDERVAN

Becoming More Than a Good Bible Study Girl
Copyright © 2009 by Lysa TerKeurst

Requests for information should be addressed to:
Zondervan, *Grand Rapids, Michigan 49530*

Library of Congress Cataloging-in-Publication Data

TerKeurst, Lysa.
    Becoming more than a good Bible study girl / Lysa TerKeurst.
      p.   cm.
    Includes bibliographical references.
    ISBN 978-0-310-29325-5 (softcover)
    1. Christian women—Religious life. 2. Christian life. 3. Spiritual life. I. Title.
BV4527.T455 2009
248.8'43—dc22
                                                  2009009945

Any Internet addresses (websites, blogs, etc.) and telephone numbers printed in this book are offered as a resource. They are not intended in any way to be or imply an endorsement by Zondervan, nor does Zondervan vouch for the content of these sites and numbers for the life of this book.

Published in association with the literary agency of Fedd & Company, Inc., 9759 Concord Pass, Brentwood, TN 37027.

Interior design: Michelle Espinoza.

Printed in the United States of America

10 11 12 13 14 15 16 • 27 26 25 24 23 22 21 20 19 18 17 16 15 14 13 12 11 10

To Holly Good, who gracefully personifies this message.

CONTENTS

PART 4

BECOMING MORE THAN A GOOD BIBLE STUDY GIRL
IN MY STRUGGLES

PART 5

BECOMING MORE THAN A GOOD BIBLE STUDY GIRL
IN MY THOUGHTS

PART 6

BECOMING MORE THAN A GOOD BIBLE STUDY GIRL
IN MY CALLING

ACKNOWLEDGMENTS

To the man who still gives me butterflies: Art. Thank you for giving me the encouragement to spread my wings and jump. When I fly, you cheer me on. And when I fall, you're always there to catch me. I love doing life with you.

To my five priority blessings: Jackson, Mark, Hope, Ashley, and Brooke. Even if I would have never gotten this message published, I would have still written it just for you. This is my heart. This is my message.

To the girls who know me, encourage me on "those days," and understand the crucial need for girls' nights out: Holly, Renee, LeAnn, Genia, Shari, and Suzy.

To Esther Fedorkevich: "Thank you" doesn't even come close to being enough for all the many ways you have stood with me. While I call you my agent, the truth is you are one of my favorite friends.

To Rob and Ashley Eagar: Thanks for helping start some wildfires with my message and ministry. I'm your biggest fan.

To the beautiful women who make Proverbs 31 Ministries what it is: LeAnn Rice, Renee Swope, Holly Good, Teri Bucholtz, Janet Burke, Lisa Clark, Terri McCall, Samantha Reed, Bonnie Schulte, Jill Tracey, Kristen Sigmon, Barb Spencer, Laurie Webster, Wendy Blight, Shari Braendel, Micca Campbell, Whitney Capps, Amy Carroll, Melanie Chitwood, Lynn Cowell, Karen Ehman, Suzie Eller, Zoe Elmore, Sharon Glasgow, Charlene Kidd, Tracie Miles, Rachel Olsen, Wendy Pope, Luann Prater, Susanne Scheppmann, Melissa Taylor, Van Walton, Marybeth Whalen, and Glynnis Whitwer.

To my bloggy friends and bloggy prayer warriors: You bless me and encourage me with your comments! I have learned so much from you, and look forward to seeing what you have to say every day. Thank you for praying this book into existence.

To the Zondervan team: Sandy Vander Zicht, Greg Clouse, Marianne Filary, Ginia Hairston, Marcy Schorsch, Michelle Lenger, Beth Shagene, John Raymond, Robin Phillips, Mike Cook, and T.J. Rathbun. Thank you for believing in this message and seeing it worthy of the Zondervan name. What a joy to be part of your family.

INTRODUCTION

This is for all three of you who like to read introductions.

Since we will be spending quite a bit of time together as you read this book, I thought it might be helpful to let you in on a little secret: I'm a very picky book reader. When I pick up a book, I don't do it lightly. It takes time to read a book, and time is a hot commodity. I'm not into wasting it. Unless, of course, I happen to be fortunate enough to be somewhere that requires me to have suntan lotion and a skirted tankini. But even then, I'm not into reading books full of theory but lacking in real-life application.

The reality is I've got dishes to wash, loads of laundry to fold, kids to raise, a ministry to run, and cellulite to deal with. If I'm going to give a book my time, I want to know that I'll be able to relate to the author as a trusted friend and that it contains a message that will challenge and impact me. If that's what I want as a reader, you better believe I want to deliver that as a writer.

So what is the message I'm delivering in this book? I want to help women not only know God's truth but also feel equipped to live it out in their everyday lives. For too many years I was full of Bible knowledge with no idea how to let the truths I knew impact my daily life. I would go to Bible study, leave all inspired, and then come home and have a complete meltdown over spilling bleach on my favorite shirt. Or a kid's bad attitude. Or finding out a friend betrayed me. Or gaining back the five pounds over a weekend that took me two months to lose.

How do we apply truth to this kind of everyday stuff? We are quick to say all the right Jesus answers in church, around our Christian friends, and in our Bible study. But when the strains of life press against us, do we live as if Jesus really works?

I'm challenged by this. And so I write not as an expert who has achieved a life that authentically reflects Jesus at all times, but as a friend who dares to try to become more than just a good Bible study girl.

Inviting you to accept this challenge is the whole point of my book. I started with a question that many people seem to be asking today. They used to ask, "Is Jesus true?" Books were written about it, sermons were preached about it, seminaries offered courses — all offering up spiritual, emotional, historical, and biblical answers proving that Jesus is true. And I gladly stand up on my kitchen chair with the paint chipping off, shouting "Hallelujah! He is the way, the truth, and the life as He claimed He was."

But now that question has shifted to, "Does Jesus work?" It's great that He's true, but what kind of difference can He make in my life? At first, this question seems bold and self-centered, not even worth answering. I would never want to reduce Jesus to the same qualifications by which I judge a car ... that's great that it's the nicest vehicle on the road, but will it get me where I want to go? Still, "Does Jesus work?" is an honest question deserving an honest answer. The world is literally dying to know.

That's why I decided to tackle six issues that each play a vital role in determining whether or not Jesus works:

- Will Jesus make a difference in my heart?
- Will He help my connection with God be more real?
- What kind of difference could He make in my relationships?
- How do I process my struggles with Jesus?
- What do I do when my thoughts pull me away from Jesus?
- Does Jesus really have a calling for my life?

If we can truthfully answer these questions as I address them one by one in the six sections of the book, I believe we'll truthfully answer the bigger "Does Jesus work?" question as well.

So, if you're looking for another "keep on keeping on" book for your bookshelf, if you're looking for a little more kumbaya in your life, or a good Jesus feeling, or how to play the Christian game better, read elsewhere. But if you, like me, want to break free from the confines of our Christian arenas and replace the world's emptiness with true fulfillment, read on.

Part 1

BECOMING MORE THAN A GOOD BIBLE STUDY GIRL

IN MY HEART

Lysa, I think you take this God thing a little too seriously!" someone once said to me.

Never have I gotten a more thrilling comment—especially because at one time I wanted nothing to do with God. It has taken me years to truly understand how to pursue God with all my heart. Not that I get it right all the time, but my deepest desire is to love God and let His love work through me to positively impact those around me.

Everywhere I go, I see women from different walks of life, and I challenge myself to *really* see them. Not just look at them—but pause to see them. And what I see often breaks my heart.

Even now as I type this in a small coffee shop, a young woman sitting at the next table pines away for the acceptance of the young man with her. She giggles, asks questions, and subtly hints at what she hopes he'll tell her. Her heart is longing for answers no man will ever be able to supply.

The heart of a woman is not only deep and wondrous but tender and vulnerable. Life can be rough on a woman when her heart gets snagged, entangled, broken, and sometimes shattered in ways beyond repair. Maybe you've been there. I have.

In this section, I want to address those things that pull our hearts away from the intimacy God desires with us. We'll journey through the feelings that we're not good enough and discover what a lie that is! Then we'll uncover the myth that the things of this world can fill up the gaps in our soul. And finally, we'll peek behind the haunting question that holds many of us hostage, "Do I really measure up?"

It's about to get messy here because that's the way honesty can be. We're not after plastic Christian answers. We're seeking more than that. So much more. So, for the sake of our hearts, let's go. Let's dare to ask what might happen if we were to become more than just good Bible study girls in our hearts.

Chapter 1

TRYING TO BE GOOD ENOUGH

I'm not sure when I first felt I wasn't good enough, but my earliest stinging memory of it happened while tumbling about a skating rink full of elementary school kids. I was a fifth grader wrapped in a less-than-desirable package. My mind's eye could see gorgeous possibilities for my frizzy brown hair and buck teeth. If only my mother would let me dye my hair blonde and get it professionally straightened, if only I could convince my dentist to replace my crooked teeth with gleaming false ones perfectly sized and aligned, my world would be wonderful. The boys would start sending me notes with little boxes for me to check yes or no. I would be confident and fulfilled.

But my mother had neither the money nor the vision for my plan. So, there I sat watching the cute boys couple skating with the cute girls while Rick Springfield's smooth but edgy voice belted out "Jessie's Girl." (And for those of you who are wondering who in the world Rick Springfield is, I am so sad you missed out on the delight called '80s music.)

I fidgeted with the laces on my skates hoping to send a very clear message: the only reason I wasn't couple skating was that I had a slight equipment malfunction. But in my heart, a false perception was cutting deeper and deeper into my soul with every beat of the Rick Springfield song.

The false perception was rooted in this one flawed thought: *You, Lysa, are not acceptable the way you are.*

Have you ever let that flawed self-perception negatively affect you? It sent me into an identity crisis as my mind swirled with possible solutions: *Since you aren't acceptable, you must find some things upon which to hitch your identity. Since it is not possible for you to be "Lysa, the cute girl," you must become something else.*

"Lysa, the smart girl." Or maybe "Lysa, the responsible girl."

"Lysa, the rebel." "Lysa, the good friend." "Lysa, the dork." "Lysa, the student body president." "Lysa, the loser."

Lost in a flood of thoughts, I saw these labels less and less like opportunities and more and more like prison cells. People label and categorize so they can define who fits where and with whom, but I had neither the spiritual depth nor the mental maturity to break free. So, trying to become more acceptable, more worthy, more loveable became my pattern, and worrying about what others thought of me a consuming, often condemning way of doing life. Their opinions were my measuring stick by which to answer the question, "Who am I?"

LOST IN LABELS

Eventually the frizzy-haired, buck-toothed girl grew into a young woman. Braces had fixed the teeth. And "the bigger, the better" styles of the '80s proved kind to people with hair like mine. I had boys asking me out and, thanks to a silly pop culture book called *The Official Preppy Handbook*, I figured out my own version of being cool. Life was finally lining up as I had always dreamed it would. Only I still didn't feel secure in who I was. The things I tried to do to define my identity kept shifting. I was someone's girlfriend, but then we would break up. I was a good student, but then I'd make a bad grade. I was responsible, but then I pulled a stupid stunt and wrecked my car. Who I thought I was one day fell apart the next.

On top of my adolescent issues, I also was haunted by hurts from my childhood. When I was eight years old, a man who was like a grandfather sexually abused me over a period of three years. Then, when I was eleven, my father walked out on my mother, my sister, and me. I felt totally abandoned. My parents wound up divorcing, and my mom was forced to work two jobs to try to make ends meet. These events left me completely lost.

Desperate to help my sister and me, one Sunday my mom announced we'd be adding a little churchgoing to our life's equation. So, with a dress and a Bible we headed off to the large, white-steepled building. I liked the idea of having a religion and having the rules of the Christian game so clearly laid out before me. It was like God was a vending machine. I put in what was required, and then He was supposed to give me what rule-following people deserved. As long as I kept up my end of the deal, God would bless me. I became "Lysa, the good girl."

Life settled a bit. My mom eventually got remarried to a wonderful man who loved me and my sister as his own. They decided to have more children, which completely thrilled the entrepreneurial spirit within me. Babysitting jobs abounded, and my parents paid well.

My sister and I welcomed a sister a few days after my fifteenth birthday. Then another sister was born the day of my senior prom. I got all dressed in my long black gown, fixed my hair extra big, donned a rhinestone necklace, slipped a flower corsage around my wrist, then headed to the maternity ward to greet my mom and my newest baby sister. What a great pre-prom activity, if you know what I mean. We got off the elevator right at the nursery window and peeked in at all those products of love.

I'll never forget seeing Haley for the first time. She had beautiful, big, blue eyes and black hair curling in every direction. I loved each of my sisters, but the minute I saw Haley my heart melted as never before. Maybe it was because I was eighteen and technically old enough to be her mother. Certainly the summer that followed found me toting Haley around as if she were my very own.

Soon it was time to pack up and head for college. I said my good-byes, lingering a little longer over Haley. With my trusty electric-blue

Firebird packed to the brim, and my parents following closely behind, we made the eight-hour trip to my new home away from home.

I saw college as the chance to completely reinvent who I was. No one there knew of my nerdy past, my absent father, the horrendous abuse, or my lack of a skating partner in the fifth grade. So I became what I thought would bring me great fulfillment and happiness: "Lysa, the popular sorority girl dating the popular football player."

At last I had it all. I had love and beauty, popularity and success, freedom and a plan for my future. Oh yes, and I had my religion.

THE FAILURE OF RELIGION

Then one night I got a call from my mom that changed everything. Her urgent tone made my pulse race and my hands shake. Haley was sick. Very sick.

I drove through the night, and by the time I got to the hospital, Haley was in the intensive care unit. My parents had been told that her liver was failing and she would not survive without a transplant. I kicked into high gear making deals with God. That's what religious people do, I reasoned. *I'll be better. I'll follow the rules more closely. I'll be kinder. I'll give more to the church. I'll attend more regularly. I'll sacrifice whatever You require, God ... just save my sister.*

Haley was transferred to a children's hospital in another state, where shortly thereafter she received a new liver. She made it through the first scary, post-surgery days and soon seemed to be completely on the mend. God was answering my prayers!

Since summer had arrived again, I was able to spend quite a bit of time with Haley as she recuperated. Weeks passed, Haley grew stronger every day, and the time came for me to head back to college for my sophomore year.

I remember well my last night in the hospital with her. Wanting to memorize all of her features, I let my eyes trace every detail. I kissed her chubby cheeks and her small, cold feet. I placed my finger against her hand and watched as each of her fingers curled around mine. And I prayed more deals with God. Deals that involved me getting to have many more nights to rock her and sing lullabies in the dark.

Then it was time to go. With one last promise to visit real soon, I returned to my college life.

Back at school, I called my mom every morning to ask how Haley was doing. Her progress continued. I was keeping up my end of the bargain with God, and He was keeping His. Religion was indeed a fine addition to my life.

But my view of religion and rule-following and making deals with God shattered two weeks afterward. I'd called my mom as usual that morning to ask about Haley. My mom was silent. Not understanding, I asked the question again ... and again. Finally, in a voice so slight I could barely hear her, she whispered, "Haley is finally all better, Lysa. She went to be with Jesus this morning."

Anger I never knew existed erupted from some deep place within me. Life's unfairness strained against my religious perceptions and the dam of my soul burst wide open. I snapped. With my fist raised toward heaven, I vowed I would never love God, serve God, or believe in God again. I had tried to be good enough to earn His love but just as my earthly daddy had done, I felt as though my heavenly Father just turned away. "Lysa, the good girl" would no longer be my identity.

My flawed ideas of God would only let me love Him when He did good things. I couldn't compute how He could have let Haley die. Other heartbreaking things had happened in my life, but this was different. The other things I'd been through were caused by flawed people. But Haley's death couldn't be pinned on a person. God had allowed it. He heard my cries. He watched me promise her everything would be okay as I sang her those lullabies. He saw her pain. And He just let her die? I could not sort through this and find anything that made sense.

At Haley's funeral, I remember mentally closing my heart off to God, letting my hurt and disillusionment take over. The thought that

I wasn't good enough was more than just a feeling. It had become the filter through which I processed life.

My daddy couldn't love me.

God couldn't love me.

I was desperate to be loved.

So, I found men who told me they loved me.

The thought that I wasn't good enough was more than just a feeling. It had become the filter through which I processed life.

Until then, I'd saved myself for marriage. It was a religious rule I'd carefully followed. But my bitterness toward God numbed my conscience and helped pave the way for rejecting many of my religious convictions. Life became a wild party full of temporary moments of happiness. The deeper I sank into this lifestyle, the more desperate I felt. It wasn't long before I found myself sitting in an abortion clinic realizing I'd made a terrible mess of my life. Now I was "Lysa, the girl who walked away from God and had an abortion." I went home that day horrified at who I'd become.

MY BIBLE FRIEND

Ironically, at this time when I was so very far from God, I had a close friend who loved the Lord with every fiber of her being. I not so affectionately referred to her as my "Bible friend," because she got on my nerves with her constant Scripture quoting. No matter what issue someone had, she was ready with a verse to help. Have a headache? She had a verse for that. Break up with your boyfriend? She had a verse for that too. I would have dreams of her chasing me around ready to whack me on the head with her very large Bible.

But something about her made me want to remain friends with her. Though her Scripture quoting could be annoying, something about it was endearing, the purest form of honesty. In addition, she modeled what it meant to live the Word and not just quote it. There was a stark difference between religion as I understood it and what she called her relationship with God.

Though she had no idea of the junk I was dealing with, she was tenderly responsive to God's promptings. One especially dark and tearful day, I received a card from her. It would have been my due date. The day I would have been welcoming a new life into the world was filled with feelings of death, darkness, and hopelessness. I knew as soon as I saw the handwriting what would be in store for me if I opened the envelope ... another Bible verse. Sure enough, Jeremiah 29:11 was beautifully scripted across the front of the card: "'For I know the plans I have for you,' declares the LORD, 'plans to prosper you and not to harm you, plans to give you hope and a future.'"

I wanted to toss the card aside, but something kept me focused on that verse. I read it over and over again. It was as if my name had been inserted there. "Lysa, for I know the plans I have for you, plans to prosper you and not to harm you, Lysa. Plans to give you, Lysa, a hope and a future."

How could this be? This statement stood in such stark contrast to my flawed perception of being identified by my circumstances. This verse painted a possibility that the God of the universe loved me not for what I did right but simply because I was His. A child for whom He had great things planned. I didn't have to be the child of a broken parent; I could be a child of God.

In that moment I didn't know how to properly accept Jesus. I didn't know the right Scriptures to turn to. Even if I did have a list of verses to pray through, I wouldn't have been able to find them in the Bible. I didn't have all the answers, and I knew for certain I had not been "good enough." But something deep in my soul was stirring with assurance that this message was from God Himself and His words in this verse were truth.

Even an atheistic heart like mine couldn't run from this truth. When God made me, He left His mark deep inside. His fingerprints covered my soul no wonder His truth resonated within me. I simply couldn't deny it. There was just one word I knew must be uttered in response to the God of the universe, pausing in this moment just for me.

"Yes."

Wrapped in that yes was the acknowledgment that God did exist, that He loved me, and that I wanted Him — not a religion — in my life in a way I'd never had before. I wanted so much more with God.

It would take me many years to completely define and understand everything that yes meant. We'll get to more of my story as this book unfolds. But the initial yes was a step toward God. A step out of the darkness that blinded me. A step toward the light of truth. A step toward my true identity that wouldn't shift or fall apart under life's strains. A step toward becoming "Lysa, a fulfilled child of the one true God."

Interestingly enough, the rest of that verse shook my soul to attention: "Then you will call upon me and come and pray to me, and I will listen to you. You will seek me and find me when you seek me with all your heart" (Jeremiah 29:12 – 13). The words "I will listen to you" and "you will find me" made God seem so personal, so touchable, so interested in a relationship with me. Me? The child of a father who didn't want me or love me is loved and wanted by the mightiest of kings, the Lord of all lords, the God of the universe, my heavenly Father!

BEYOND THE CHRISTIAN CHECKLIST

Learning to seek God with all of your heart is what I hope you are inspired to do as you move forward. Seeking with all of your heart requires more than just the routine Christian good girl checklist:

- ✔ Pray.
- ✔ Read the Bible.
- ✔ Do a Bible study.
- ✔ Go to church.

✔ Be nice.
✔ Don't hold a grudge against boys who didn't ask you to couple skate in the fifth grade.

Okay, well maybe that last one is just my issue. But you catch my drift.

Seeking with all of your heart requires more than just the routine Christian good girl checklist.

I want my life with Jesus to be fulfilling. I want my beliefs to work no matter what life throws at me. I want to be so certain of God's presence that I never feel like I have to face anything in my own strength or rely on my own perspectives. My strength will weaken during hard times. My perspectives get skewed by my emotions.

I want total security no matter what happens. In other words, I want my relationship with Jesus to be enough to keep me sane and together and still fully devoted. Is this possible? True fulfillment no matter what?

Fulfillment means to be completely satisfied. How might our lives look if we were so filled with God's truths we could let go of the pain of our past, not get tripped up by the troubles of today, or consumed by worries about tomorrow? Sound impossible? It *is* impossible when we try to make it happen on our own by doing more good Bible study girl things. Praying, reading the Bible, doing another Bible study, going to church, and being nice are wonderful and necessary. But just going through the motions of these activities will not fill our souls. They must be done with the great expectation and heart cry for God to lead us into a deeper and more life-changing connection with Him.

Ask a group of Christian women what makes them feel fulfilled and chances are they'll answer you with things that they do. But true fulfillment is never found in seeking to do enough, be enough, have enough, know enough, or accomplish enough. "Enough" is elusive, always just slightly out of reach. Many of us know this, but still we continue the same patterns of trying to be good Bible study girls—hoping that if we do it long enough, fulfillment will somehow fall within our grasp.

It is my prayer that reading this book will help you to discover two things: (1) a more meaningful connection with God, and (2) a truer fulfillment from letting your relationship with Him transform every area of your life. Though it may seem a pretty lofty goal, will you pray for them with me: "God, will You help me to have a deeper connection with You and find truer fulfillment as You transform every area of my life. That is the cry and desire of my heart." You might even want to add these four simple requests that go right alongside having a deeper connection with God:

> *God, I want to see You.*
> *God, I want to hear You.*
> *God, I want to know You.*
> *So that I can follow hard after You every day.*

I originally wrote that prayer in my book *What Happens When Women Say Yes to God*, but I think it is worth carrying over here. It will help us daily set our hearts and minds in the right place as we not only read this book but start to live its truths. Colossians 3:1–2 encourages us, "Since, then, you have been raised with Christ, set your hearts on things above, where Christ is seated at the right hand of God. Set your minds on things above, not on earthly things." Setting our hearts and our minds on God and letting His truths change us, rearrange us, and redirect us will help us not just to know the message of Christ—but to live it out!

And with that wonderful assurance, we are off. Do you happen to have any Rick Springfield songs downloaded on your iPod that we could play as we continue on our journey?

Chapter 2

FLITTING TO AND FRO

I couldn't quite land. That's the way I felt after I said yes to God but then started trying to figure out what I was supposed to do with my life. I wanted to make a difference for Him, but couldn't figure out what I had to offer. I was like an unwilling feather — weightless, exhausted from all the flitting to and fro, but completely unable to resist the winds that carried me away.

When I thought about all that filled my life as a woman in her early twenties, everything I ever thought would make me feel happy stared back at me. A diploma, a husband, a child, a minivan, and a house with the appropriate seasonal foliage were all there. That's what made the hollow feeling in my chest especially troublesome.

This emptiness made me feel desperate, needy, complicated, full of unrealistic expectations. I quickly became disillusioned. Weren't Christians supposed to instantly have it all together after saying yes to God? My relationships with my husband and growing family were strained and quickly went from being blessings to burdens. Even though I knew in my head that only God could fill my soul, I still found myself wanting my husband and kids to do the job. It just seemed easier trying to get these things from those I could see and touch. But even a great husband and wonderful kids made very poor gods. They couldn't possibly do what I was asking of them.

Wanting inner peace so badly, I started searching for something to do that might make me feel significant.

CAREER CRAZY

A crazy magazine article I read suggested I could find myself by identifying my inner beauty and exploring it out in the world of work and career. So I took my inner self and headed to the community college to take a class on floral design. Things went well in the class because we worked mainly with silk flowers. However, once I was hired at a real floral shop, my inner beauty calling failed me. The overwhelming scent of all those flowers in a small, enclosed space overstimulated my gag reflex. And, really, nothing draws in the customers more than a young designer who gags a lot.

With my calling as a floral designer in grave jeopardy, my career search continued. I came across a flyer that offered a correspondence course in bridal consulting. The pitch basically translated like this: "Send us your money and we'll send you a certificate that says you know what you're doing." I could have a new career as easy as that! The thing that totally made me feel legitimate was that my certificate had a gold seal on it. You can't just buy those anywhere, you know.

Off I went into the world of edgy brides, overbearing mothers, overspent fathers, and terrified grooms. I would have had a shot at this career had it not been for my queasy aversion to neurotic people. Right before my first bride was supposed to walk down the aisle, I made a mad dash for the church parking lot, where I slumped over and lost my lunch between a gardenia bush and the visitor parking sign. As the mother of the bride came flying toward me—ready to beat me with the broomstick I imagined must be nearby—I was struck by how welcoming that visitor sign looked and how this might be a church I'd like to attend some time. Well, except for the fact that every time I walked through the parking lot I'd remember the most ungracious gift I'd left there. I decided I probably wouldn't take advantage of their generous parking offer. Nor would I continue planning weddings.

My next career adventure led me to kitchen gadget sales. It made perfect sense, really. I hated to cook and didn't have a clue about how to navigate my way around a kitchen. I'm just logical that way.

I quickly became a master at making stuff up to cover my culinary ignorance. If customers asked why I didn't first peel the outer layer of the onion before using it, I told them peeling was very "old school" and studies now showed that the peel contained all the nutrients. I have since discovered this to be true of potatoes, so I wasn't that far off.

I was quite far off, however, in my failure to read the directions for the proper use and care of some of the more dangerous tools I demonstrated. Hence the explanation why this career also came to an abrupt end. I may or may not have bled on a certain vegetable pizza after an unfortunate encounter with a slicer. This pizza was still served, mind you, and helped end my brief aspiration to become a chef who was pampered.

One day I came home and told my husband about a meeting I'd had with a friend of mine who asked me to help with a newsletter called *Proverbs 31*. He gave me a look that said, "And how long will this little career tangent last?" Clearly, he had not read the part of Proverbs 31 that describes a husband's option to go to the city gate and sing his wife's praises. But to be honest, I hadn't read it either. In fact, I was with the ministry for three months before it ever dawned on me to actually read that chapter in Proverbs.

When I finally did read Proverbs 31, I felt just as much an imposter as I had in my kitchen gadget days. Who was I to be working with a Christian ministry? Especially a ministry that taught women to love their husbands, nurture their children, and follow after God every day? None of this seemed truly possible for me. I was a hollow woman, not a holy woman. I had said yes to Jesus being my Savior, but didn't have a clue how He could be the answer to my emptiness.

FAILED REMEDIES AND FALSE GODS

As a little girl, I had longed for a daddy to pick me up, swing me around, and tell me I was lovely and loved. When this childhood longing went unmet, it became an adult emptiness and brokenness that drove me to seek out all kinds of misguided remedies. My primary remedy was to look for someone or something that would make me feel loved and significant. It's as if I carried around a little heart-shaped cup and extended it to whatever or whomever I perceived might fill it.

I presented the cup to my education: "Will you fill me?"

I offered it to my husband: "Will you fill me?"

I held it out to my children: "Will you fill me?"

I extended it to my material possessions: "Will you fill me?"

I presented it to each of my jobs: "Will you fill me?"

Within these questions were many more entanglements: "Will you right all my wrongs?" "Will you fill up my insecurities?" "Will you make me feel significant?" The more I offered my emptiness hoping something could fill it, the more frustrated I felt. And now that I'd said yes to God, I was especially perplexed. Wasn't this Christian thing supposed to fix these kinds of issues in my heart? What was I missing? Have you ever been there?

The reality is no person, possession, profession, or position ever fills the cup of a wounded, empty heart—not my heart, not your heart. It's an emptiness only God can fill. Anything we use as a substitute for God is an idol, a false god. I didn't know it at the time, but it's a truth splashed in vivid color throughout the pages of Scripture. Perhaps the most dramatic story takes place in 1 Kings 18—the showdown between the prophet Elijah and the 450 prophets of Baal.

No person, possession, profession, or position ever fills the cup of a wounded, empty heart.

Elijah has challenged the people of Israel to choose whom they will serve—the true God or the idol Baal. When they say nothing in response, he throws down the gauntlet to King Ahab and the prophets of Baal. Each side will build an altar, sacrifice a bull, and call on their deity to rain down fire and consume the sacrifice. The deity who responds with fire is the one the people will accept as God. The prophets of Baal go first:

> *So they took the bull given them and prepared it. Then they called on the name of Baal from morning till noon. "O Baal, answer us!" they shouted. But there was no response; no one answered. And they danced around the altar they had made.*
>
> *At noon Elijah began to taunt them. "Shout louder!" he said. "Surely he is a god! Perhaps he is deep in thought, or busy, or traveling. Maybe he is sleeping and must be awakened." So they shouted louder and slashed themselves with swords and spears, as was their custom, until their blood flowed. Midday passed, and they continued their frantic prophesying until the time for the evening sacrifice. But there was no response, no one answered, no one paid attention. (1 Kings 18:26–29)*

Reread that last sentence again: "But there was no response, no one answered, no one paid attention." It's a vivid picture and a strong warning, and the same response we'll get whenever we try to get our fulfillment from a false god—from anyone or anything apart from the one true God.

The triumphant conclusion to this story is that God sends a consuming bolt of fire that devours Elijah's altar. The people of Israel repent and the prophets of Baal are slaughtered. The one true God—our God—was made known that day. Our God responded. Our God answered. Our God paid attention. He always does.

Do you have an empty, heart-shaped cup? If so, what have you asked to fill it in the past? What might you be asking to fill it right now? I've matured in this area and yet can still find myself slipping back at times. Why is it so tempting to look to things of this world for fulfillment?

This notion that worldly things can fulfill is all around us. It's on TV, the focus of countless secular songs (even those '80s songs I heart so much ... hmmm). I can't even go to the grocery store checkout lane without being bombarded with suggestions for a more fulfilling life. A better sex life. A better career. A more beautifully decorated house. The magazines seem so slick, their promises so enticing. And they *do* bring temporary excitement. But every single thing the world offers is temporary. These fixes can never fill our void long-term.

BATTLING THE "IF ONLY I HAD" TEMPTATION

Even if we don't fall into the idolatry of relying *solely* on other people or things to fill us, we can still be tempted by the lie that the things of this world bring fulfillment. It's a lie that typically goes something like this: *I could really be happy and fulfilled if only I had ...*

... a skinnier body.
... a husband.
... a husband who was more tender and romantic.
... more money.
... a more successful career.
... a better personality.
... a baby.
... smarter kids.

I don't know what your "if only I had" statements are, but I do know that none of them will bring fulfillment. Becoming more than a good Bible study girl means realizing that, apart from a thriving relationship with God, even if you got everything on your list, there would still be a hollow gap in your soul.

Instead of saying, "If only I had...." and filling in the blank with some person, possession, profession, or position, make a choice to replace that statement with something that draws your heart into God's truth. Since we cannot be pulled away from God and draw near to Him at the same time, speaking truth rights our perspectives and puts our focus where it should be.

Here are some examples that have helped me battle the temptation to let people, possessions, or position take God's place in my life.

PEOPLE

I no longer say, "If only I would have had a daddy who loved me. . . ." Instead, I say, "Psalm 68:5 promises God will be a father to the fatherless. I don't have to be the child of a broken family my whole life. I can be a child of God. God can fill in every gap left by my father and use what I learned through that experience for good."

Maybe your gap wasn't left by an absent father but by a friend who hurt you. Or perhaps a husband who left you. Or the children you've longed to have but still don't. Whatever that gap is, God is the perfect fit for your emptiness. Pray this paraphrase of Luke 1:78–79: "Because of the tender mercy of my God by which the rising sun will come to me from heaven — to shine on my darkness and in what feels like the shadow of death to me — I will find peace."

POSSESSIONS

I no longer say, "If only I had more possessions. . . ." Instead, I recite Matthew 6:19–21: "Do not store up for yourselves treasures on earth, where moth and rust destroy, and where thieves break in and steal. But store up for yourselves treasures in heaven, where moth and rust do not destroy, and where thieves do not break in and steal. For where your treasure is, there your heart will be also."

Any possession I ever long for, no matter how good it may seem, will only be good for a limited time. In light of eternity, every possession is in the process of breaking down, becoming devalued, and will eventually be taken from us. If I set my heart solely on acquiring more and more things, I'll feel more and more vulnerable with the possibility of loss.

Possessions are meant to be appreciated and used to bless others; they were never meant to be identity markers. It's not wrong to enjoy the possessions we have as long as we don't depend on them for our heart's security.

POSITION

I no longer say, "If only I had a better position...." Instead, I recite the words of Psalm 119:105: "Your word is a lamp to my feet and a light for my path." I don't need a better position to get where I should go. I don't have to figure out my path and jockey to get ahead. I need God's Word to guide me. Only as I follow Him and honor Him step by step can I be assured that I'm right where He wants me to be doing what He wants me to do.

Whatever "if only I had" statement you are struggling with, you can replace it with solid truths from Scripture that will never leave you empty. It's a bold statement to make and might even sound a bit trite, but it's true. When God's Word gets inside of us, it becomes the new way we process life. It rearranges our thoughts, our motives, our needs, and our desires. Our soul was tailor-made to be filled with God and His truth; therefore, it seeps into every part of us and fills us completely. It is the only perfect fit. And according to Psalm 119:30–32, being filled with God's Word sets our hearts free! "I have chosen the way of the truth; I have set my heart on your laws. I hold fast to your statutes, O LORD; do not let me be put to shame. I run in the path of your commands, for you have set my heart free."

FROM CAREER TO CALLING

In the end, much to my husband's surprise, I did land and stick with a career for more than a couple of months. In fact, when I began working with Proverbs 31 Ministries I discovered something even better than a career; I discovered my calling. Working with Proverbs 31 Ministries has been one of the most thrilling faith rides I could have ever imagined. But even with the many things I've had the opportunity to do, it all pales in comparison to the relationship with God I've gained along the way. As long as I daily make the choice to be guided by His truth, He replaces my hollowness with a wholeness of love that has no gaps.

And with that fullness from God, I can put away that heart-shaped cup I used during all those needy years. Instead of always looking to get fulfillment from my loved ones and the other blessings in my life, I can simply enjoy them for what they are.

As long as I daily make the choice to be guided by His truth, He replaces my hollowness with a wholeness of love that has no gaps.

Recently I had an experience similar to the one I described at the beginning of this chapter. This time I sat on my bed and reviewed my life. I pulled out my laptop computer and let my heart go:

I'm pausing right now.

Tears are softly sliding down my cheeks.

Art is watching a taped sporting event. I'm glad I don't know the outcome of that game ... I'd be so tempted to taunt him with possibilities, accidentally spilling the beans.

The boys are home with friends in tow. Deep voices escape their rooms with bursts of laughter. Boys quietly turning into men are playing video games tonight.

Hope is asleep in one of my bedroom chairs. Her breathing is steady. Her curls fall haphazardly around her beautiful face. Her pink polished toes are sticking out from the blanket wrapped about her. When did her feet grow big enough to wear my shoes?

Little Brooke is snuggled close on my bed with me. She was so frustrated because she wanted to swim with big sis,

Ashley, and friends. But I kept her inside with me. I'm glad I did. We snuggled and giggled and watched a movie together. She lasted four minutes into the movie before her eyes closed and sweet dreams became her entertainment.

And Ashley, now done with swimming, is flitting about the house with four great friends. The clock will strike midnight soon, and it will officially be the day she turns thirteen.

I want so desperately to freeze this moment. To drink in every sound, every sight, every delightful evidence of life. So many things to be thankful for. I've had thousands of these everyday life minutes, but tonight is different. I remembered to pause. To acknowledge what I've been blessed with. I didn't rush the kids off to bed so I could have my time. I sat and soaked in the moment. And with every tear that spilled out, I felt more and more full.

Maybe this is the true secret to being fulfilled and content. Living in the moment with God, defined by His truth, and with no unrealistic expectations for others or things to fill me up. Not reaching back for what was lost in my yesterdays. And not reaching for what I hope will be in my tomorrow. But living fully with what is right in front of me. And truly seeing the gift of this moment.

I have finally landed. That's the way I feel since I stopped that intense search for what I am supposed to become in life. I still have goals and hopes for my future, but they no longer send me into a striving frenzy. But I must continue to pursue truth that keeps me grounded and God's love that keeps me filled. Then my desperate hollowness is replaced by a desire for holiness. And though it took me years to get it, and though I definitely don't live it out perfectly, I have finally found what I'd been looking for.

Chapter 3

WHEN I FEEL LIKE I DON'T MEASURE UP

R ewarding.

That's what this particular day was supposed to be, my shining-star day at my kids' school. Finally, I was going to get the Really Good Mommy Award.

Not that this is an official award on a frame-worthy piece of fine linen paper. It is not. It's just a feeling—that feeling of getting a thumbs-up and acceptance nod that you are in fact doing an okay job as a mom.

I make it a top priority to be a good mom to my kids. But being the superstar volunteer mom at school, I'll probably never be. I've made peace with that fact. But every now and then in a moment of sheer insanity, I have visions of grandeur that send me scurrying through the craft aisles determined to at last do something noteworthy in one of my kids' classrooms.

You get the scary picture, right? One complete with glue guns, pipe cleaners, colored felt squares, unrealistic craft instructions, and one ginormous headache. Even though my spell-checker doesn't think "ginormous" is officially a word, any woman wielding craft supplies in a crowd of kids knows it is the perfect word to describe the throbbing in one's head afterward.

But this shining-star day didn't have anything to do with crafts. Nope, it was the big bake sale that was going to be my crowning glory.

I had volunteered to make 100 individually wrapped homemade brownies. And I was going to be completely fancy and use the turtle brownie mix that comes in a box as opposed to just the plain old fudge brownie mix that comes in the little economy bags. Like I said, only "homemade" would do for this project.

The recipe actually required me to break open a few eggs and measure out some water and oil. And then, using the tip of a knife just like the directions say, I even made designs with the caramel drizzle on top. I spoke out loud during the whole process so I could be well rehearsed when the *Rachael Ray Show* called wanting to feature me on their school bake sale episode. Because they often want guests who use box mixes.

"And then you place them in the perfectly preheated oven and, oh look, there is a pan ready to come out right now. Our toothpick tester comes out clean so we know they are done and ready to cool. Right after this commercial break, we'll be back with the perfect way to package up our perfect brownies, which are sure to get you all those ooohs and ahhhs you've always dreamed of."

Carefully, I cut and lifted each brownie into the safety of its own little baggie. I neatly arranged rows of brownies in a rectangular wicker basket I'd bought years ago. It was another one of those visions-of-grandeur moments when the craft store had a wicker basket sale. I could totally imagine myself wearing a clever little apron while toting casseroles in this basket down the street to a neighbor's house.

But the basket sat in a remote cabinet still sporting its sales tag and collecting dust for years. I smiled as I popped the tag off the handle and sat back to admire my hard work. One last pan of brownies to package up and I was headed to bake sale glory.

I glanced up at the clock and saw that we needed to leave for school in three minutes. Quickly I recruited my daughters to help me finish up. Brownies 94, 95, 96, and then a disaster of epic proportions occurred ... right as my oldest daughter was packaging brownie number 97.

Nuts.

These turtle brownies had nuts in them. Lots of nuts. And there I was standing over individually wrapped brownie number 97 listening to my daughter's reminder that our school is, in fact, a peanut-free school. No peanut butter crackers. No PB&J sandwiches. And certainly no nuts in the brownies at the bake sale.

Have you ever been in a situation where you felt like your head could possibly explode into a million tiny particles of pixie dust?

My arms started flailing about as if to gather the pieces of my scattered brain and tuck everything back into place. I sent the kids to the car and ate brownies 98, 99, and 100.

I pulled out the school handbook to get the coordinator's phone number, and in big, bold letters the words, "We are a peanut-free school" jumped out and mocked all of my best intentions. I called and left the dreaded message that I, in fact, would not be bringing my bake sale items to the school that day.

No shining star. No Really Good Mommy Award. No ooohs and ahhhs over my rectangular wicker basket filled to the brim with the deliciousness known as the turtle brownie. No happy, proud kids elated with their mom's efforts.

Just a little caramel crust resting above my quivering lip and ninety-seven individually wrapped brownies. With nuts, no less.

I spent the rest of the day trying to process the great brownie failure of 2008. At first, I saw it as a debacle that defined my motherhood journey. Grand visions that led to big messes that led to unmet expectations that heaped more and more guilt on my already slightly fragile motherhood psyche.

In the grand scheme of life, this was not a big deal. I realize that now. But in the moment, it felt huge. With apologies once again to the spell-checker, it felt ginormous.

Suddenly I was overcome by a tidal wave of memories recalling many other events in which I'd fallen short. The more I let my mind free-fall into the pit of negativity and shame, the more disabled I felt.

And that's exactly where Satan would have loved for me to stay. That's his daily goal, actually. If Satan can use our everyday experiences, both big and small, to cripple our true identity, then he renders God's people totally ineffective for the kingdom of Christ.

These were brownies.

For a school bake sale.

And these brownies had somehow knocked me to the ground. I didn't want to smile. I didn't want to be kind. I didn't want to be a disciple for Christ that day.

If Satan can use our everyday experiences, both big and small, to cripple our true identity, then he renders God's people totally ineffective for the kingdom of Christ.

I wanted to drive to school too fast, turn into the parking lot on two wheels, get out of my vehicle (the one with a logo of my husband's Christian business proudly displayed on the side), and scream at the top of my lungs, "Whoever's idea this was to have a bake sale today is officially no longer my friend! Do you see what this crazy bake sale has done to me? I will just give you the whole $10 you might have made if you could have sold my 100 individually wrapped, homemade-from-a-box, turtle brownie squares. And did I mention that I have 100 individually wrapped brownie squares at home? Make that ninety-seven squares. Ninety-seven squares of chocolate deliciousness on a day in which a bake sale has sent my hormones raging!"

Note that I said I *wanted* to do that. I didn't. But I must admit, the tailspin of not measuring up isn't a pretty sight.

If you can relate to any of this story, this chapter is for you. If you can't, you are totally free to skip this part and go make some extra homemade deliciousness for those of us that will show up at the bake sale tomorrow without our goodies. We heart you. And we thank you in advance.

Now back to the rest of us who have ever felt like we came up short.

FEELING TOTALLY INADEQUATE

Satan delights in our feelings of inadequacy. He wants to help us stay there. He wants us to go to Bible study, learn the deep truths of God, leave all encouraged, and then come home and have a complete meltdown over ninety-seven brownies that didn't make the bake sale cut.

He wants us to entertain a very dangerous thought: "Why doesn't Jesus work for me?" When I let my brain run away with this line of thinking, I start wondering why Jesus didn't step in and help me remember the "no nuts" detail before it was too late. I mean, Jesus is quite capable of doing that, right? He is big and mighty, capable of moving mountains. Surely He could have stopped me from adding nuts and ruining those brownies. Maybe He just didn't care enough to stop me.

You see, if Satan can get us asking these kinds of questions, then we can easily justify distancing ourselves from God, once more reducing our relationship with Him to items on a checklist. I prayed. I gave. I served. I did my duty. Now, I hope God does His part and keeps blessing my life.

But "Why doesn't Jesus work for me?" is never the right question. Instead, when circumstances shift and we feel like we fall short, we should ask, "How can I see Jesus even in this?"

The only way I can ask myself this question is when I pull back from whatever situation I'm facing and separate my circumstance from my identity.

My circumstance in this case was supposed to be a wonderful and productive bake sale contribution that helped the school and made me feel accomplished. But my circumstance shifted, as circumstances so often do. It became a brownie mishap in which I redefined myself as a failing mom.

Ever been there?

Now let's state what is true. Despite my feelings, my identity stayed the same. I am a loving mom. I am a giving person. I am a woman who takes her responsibilities seriously.

But when my circumstances got entangled with not measuring up, I redefined my identity by thinking thoughts like, *I am an irresponsible failure who constantly lets her kids down.* This is a lie that leads me right where Satan wants me.

Becoming more than a good Bible study girl means I separate my shortcomings from my identity and let Jesus be the only measure of my worth. Separating the circumstance from my identity allows me to see the circumstance for what it is—a mistake. It doesn't mean I'm a failure as a mom; it means I was slightly disorganized about double-checking the bake sale details. Instead of using my mistake as a club to beat myself up, I can choose to see it as a call to action.

WHEN THE RIGHTEOUS FALL, THEY BOUNCE BACK

"For though a righteous man falls seven times, he rises again, but the wicked are brought down by calamity" (Proverbs 24:16). Isn't it interesting that the writer of Proverbs clearly points out that sometimes the righteous man falls? Not once, not twice, not three times, but *seven* times.

I feel bad for him. He had seven bake sale debacles. That comes out to 700 individually wrapped, homemade-from-a-box turtle brownies. Okay, I readily admit that maybe that wasn't his exact circumstance. I bet he made full-out peanut butter cookies. But his circumstance is not the point. The point is his response.

And how did he respond? He got up. He bounced back. He didn't wallow in his mistake and question his identity and peel into the school on two wheels. He kept his identity intact—he was still called righteous though he'd fallen seven times. And he got past his circumstance by seeing his shortcomings as a call to action. He got back up each time.

How did I ever see Jesus in the great brownie failure of 2008? Well, the first thing I did was to separate my identity from my failure. I failed at the task of making 100 nut-free brownies, but this doesn't make me a failure.

My call to action? Getting more intentional about writing down the details of the things I volunteered for at school. I started to print out the instructions for every project before beginning.

And I have to insert a little heart check here as well. If I am volunteering to get people's approval and striving to prove my worth by getting their compliments, then I'm setting myself up for potential disappointment every time. The reason failure hurts is because we are trying so stinkin' hard to measure up. But the way people measure each other can change frequently, based on feelings, performance, and often unrealistic expectations.

God never intended for us to rely on others for our sense of well-being. Only He is equipped to provide that. His perfectly stable, unshifting, unconditional love is the only real measure of my worthiness. Realizing that gets me back to the real heart of volunteerism, which is serving God by loving others out of the abundance of His love in me.

God never intended for us to rely on others for our sense of well-being. Only He is equipped to provide that.

My last lesson from the brownie incident was choosing to stop taking such things so seriously. There is humor to be found in almost every failure, if only we'll look for it. And when I looked, I found a great story. One that I used when asked to be the keynote speaker at the school's Volunteer Appreciation Day that very spring.

Me.

The loving, giving mom, who takes her responsibilities seriously who also happened to have a really hilarious thing happen to her when she tried to make 100 individually wrapped brownies for the school bake sale.

The crowd at the Appreciation Day roared with laughter.

Maybe there are more than three of us who deal with "shortcomings," after all.

And for people like us, we can take courage in John 15:9–11, where Jesus says, "As the Father has loved me, so have I loved you. Now remain in my love. If you obey my commands, you will remain in my love, just as I have obeyed my Father's commands and remain in his love. I have told you this so that my joy may be in you and your joy may be complete."

It's a matter of the heart. Instead of resting my heart in the unrealistic hope that others will make my joy complete, I have to rest my heart with Jesus only. Remain in Him. Obey Him. Stay faithful to keep His commands — even when I want to yell and scream and pitch a fit over nutty brownies. Then my joy will be complete. Not because I got an award or measured up in everyone else's eyes, but rather because I am secure in the fact that God loves me and must have had some good reason for allowing the great brownie debacle!

Oh, and what about all those brownies? Well, I surely wasn't going to gain 100 pounds by leaving them within my grasp for long. I started giving them away. Then I heard that a friend of mine who has six kids had broken her foot. Perfect. We put the rest of the treats in a big gift bag, attached a note of love and well wishes, and made six kids and one broken-footed mama very happy.

Although it wasn't at all how I thought things would turn out, the same word with which I started this chapter is an appropriate way to end it . . .

Rewarding.

Part 2

BECOMING MORE THAN A GOOD BIBLE STUDY GIRL

IN MY WALK WITH GOD

When I decided to follow Christ, a shift took place in my life that rattled my soul in the best kind of way. I made a commitment to "clean up my act" and "study the Bible." I had a checklist in my head that contained all the right and wrong things a Christian woman should do. And, boy, did I ever pursue trying to be a good Christian woman!

But despite all my doing, I felt hollow. I prayed, but still felt disconnected from God. I witnessed to others, but found myself fumbling with my words and concluding with an apology. I read and studied the Bible, but felt guilty when I was less than enthusiastic about doing so. I wanted to understand and apply biblical principles to my life, but I felt so very uneducated and elementary.

What was wrong with me? How could I get beyond a relationship with God that felt flat and stale and that seemed to be making little difference in my everyday life?

One day it dawned on me to ask God for more. I literally started begging Him for insights and revelations and proof that more was possible. And slowly the shift occurred. God honors the honest prayers of people desiring a richer connection with Him.

Whether you're kicking the tires and just considering this God thing, or you've been walking with God for a long time, we would all do well to desire more of Him. In this adventure of pursuing God, never will we get to the place where we've arrived.

In the next three chapters we'll discover the thrill of becoming a self-feeder, why our time with God every day is crucial, what to do when we struggle with our devotion time, and how to study the Bible so that Scriptures absolutely come alive in our lives.

As if that's not exciting enough, might I mention we'll also be discovering the biblical response should you ever find a mattress floating in the pond in your front yard. So come on, good Bible study girls, let's find out how to walk more closely with God.

Chapter 4

BEYOND SUNDAY MORNING

I was one of those kids who was always coming up with some new-fangled plan. One of my more outlandish ideas was convincing my mom to let me set up a meeting with the preacher man at the church we'd visited a few times.

We were not model members. We weren't the kind who gave and served and willingly shook everybody's hand when the pastor instructed the congregation to turn and greet each other. I hated that part. I was very content to defiantly stay seated on that hard wooden pew and use the offering envelopes to draw pictures of the people around me. I loved the big-nosed old men and the big-haired ladies. I could really crack myself up while drawing pictures of them. Soon the whole pew would be shaking from my laughter until Mama pinched me so hard I wanted to cry.

Not only were we not members, we weren't even regular attenders —a fact that probably delighted more than a few people who fell prey to my artistic renderings.

But the times we did find ourselves sitting in that big, white-steepled building distressed me. I had never been so bored in all my livelong days. My eyes got heavy and my head started to nod until the preacher man raised his voice, squinted his eyes, pounded his fist on the pulpit, and spewed 253 microdroplets of spit. His face got so red I was afraid it might explode at any minute.

That part totally entertained me. But then my stomach started growling, and all I could focus on for the rest of the sermon was what we might be having for lunch that day and whether or not my mom would loosen up her no-sugar rules and let me have a Coke. As quickly as I shed my scratchy church dress upon arriving home, I also shed any memory of what the preacher man talked about.

It seemed like a colossal waste of time. Especially in light of the fact that I had a Donny and Marie Osmond record waiting for me at home and I much preferred their music to the choir. And my dad didn't have to go. And neither did many of my friends.

However, I did have one friend who went to a church she loved. They had "children's church" where the donuts were plentiful and the orange juice was free-flowing. None of the kids had to sit in the big church. They got to go to a room with tambourines and flannel boards and candy for the winners of a sword drill. (I won't tell you what I thought a sword drill was until I went with my friend and figured it out.)

After visiting my friend's church, I came home with a fresh vision for what church should be. I could quote the verse we learned and recall the Bible story and how it applied to my life. I was so excited at my discovery that I felt compelled to share this good news with the preacher man at "our" church.

And my mom was just crazy enough to take me to this meeting. I think she thought I was going to talk to him about getting saved or baptized. If only she had clarified ahead of time, it might have prevented the six new gray hairs she surely got after that day.

There I sat across from his big oak desk swinging my Keds back and forth. With great expression and enthusiasm I presented my case for a real bonafide children's church of our own. I even assured him that it would be okay if they couldn't afford the donuts and orange juice.

The most important thing was just having somebody who could preach sermons in a way that kids could actually understand them and make them want to go home and read the Bible for themselves.

Because, really, it's a shame to wear a scratchy dress for half a weekend day and sit on a hard pew only to draw pictures, fall asleep, and count spit droplets.

Though he refrained from kicking my little hind end out the door to the curb, I'm pretty sure the preacher man never quite caught my vision. I wouldn't know. My mama thought it best for us to start visiting my friend's church after that.

Though I hadn't presented my case with the most couth in the world, I look back on the point I was trying to make and still find it to be good one. Even at my young age, and even though I wouldn't discover what it meant to have a relationship with Jesus for many years to come, I still wanted my churchgoing experience to be more than just a Sunday morning routine.

I wanted it to count for something more than just making us look good. And though the donuts, orange juice, tambourines, flannel boards, and candy for the sword drill winners were all nice touches, what I really loved was the way my friend's church made me want to go home and open the Bible for myself.

It was a seed of hope that wouldn't come to fruition until I was an adult. But it was the beginning of seeing the Bible as more than just a big, intimidating, hard-to-understand book from which only *uber*spiritual people can learn.

ARE YOU A SELF-FEEDER?

Bill Hybels, senior pastor of Willow Creek Community Church, one of America's most influential, recently did a shocking thing. He apologized.

After surveying the thousands of people who attend Willow Creek, the church discovered that their approach to growing people spiritually was fundamentally flawed. "We made a mistake," Hybels admitted. "When people became Christians, we should have started teaching them that they have to take responsibility to become 'self-feeders.' We should have taught people how to read their Bible between services, how to practice spiritual disciplines much more aggressively on their own."[1]

I couldn't agree more. Practicing spiritual disciplines more aggressively on our own is exactly what we need. But wait a minute ... aren't we seeking to be more than just good Bible study girls? Aren't we saying that people are full of spiritual knowledge, but starved of experiencing God? Yes, but true fulfillment requires a balance of both. And the responsibility for both the learning *and* experiencing should rest on our shoulders, not our church's.

Instead of looking at the ministry options our church offers and asking, "Which one will meet my needs and feed me the way I need to be fed?" we must look at our church and ask, "Where can I make a difference in the body of Christ? Where can I become a woman who applies her knowledge of the Bible? Where can I live out the message of Jesus by serving, loving, and giving?"

Instead of looking at the ministry options our church offers and asking, "Which one will meet my needs and feed me the way I need to be fed?" we must look at our church and ask, "Where can I make a difference in the body of Christ?"

How do we become, as Bill Hybels suggests, "self-feeders"?

Well, go get yourself a big ol' gooey donut and a tall glass of OJ and we'll get started. I'm just kidding. It can be a short glass of OJ.

READING AND STUDYING THE BIBLE FOR YOURSELF

Whether you've just been checking out Christianity or been a regular church attender for years, studying the Bible on your own can be intimidating at times. But we'll never grow to our full potential unless we jump in and get serious about studying Scripture. There are three things we need to do when we read and study the Bible for ourselves: pray, discover the context, and read the passage phrase by phrase.

PRAY

Becoming a self-feeder requires that we pray first and ask God to open our spiritual eyes like never before. That's what the apostle Paul is talking about when he says, "I keep asking that the God of our Lord Jesus Christ, the glorious Father, may give you the Spirit of wisdom and revelation, so that you may know him better. I pray also that the eyes of your heart may be enlightened in order that you may know the hope to which he has called you, the riches of his glorious inheritance in the saints, and his incomparably great power for us who believe" (Ephesians 1:17 – 19).

Stop right now and pray this prayer:

God, I ask now, and I'll keep asking, that You give me a Spirit of wisdom and revelation, so I can know You better. I pray that the eyes of my heart may be enlightened that I may know the hope to which You have called me, the riches of Your glorious inheritance in the saints, and Your incomparably great power for us who believe.

Once we've prayed and prepared our hearts for seeing and receiving the wisdom contained in God's Word, we're ready to focus on the text before us.

START WITH THE CONTEXT

Whenever I read and study the Bible for myself, I like to start by learning about the larger context of the particular verse or passage. The context is found by asking basic who, what, when, where, and why questions. For the Ephesians 1 passage, for instance, I want to know things like: Why is this book of the Bible called Ephesians? Who wrote this book? Why was it written?

I use the *NIV Life Application Study Bible*, which provides a lot of helpful information, including an overview for each book of the Bible. I learn that "Ephesians" were people who lived in Ephesus, one of five major cities of the Roman Empire. The book of Ephesians was a letter written by the apostle Paul about 60 AD to the church in Ephesus. Held in a Roman prison at the time, he wrote to encourage the Ephesian Christians and to remind them of the purpose of the church.

Who was the apostle Paul? To find that answer, I look in the back of my *NIV Life Application Study Bible* at what is called an "Index to Notes." There I find all the page numbers in my Bible with commentary about Paul. Commentaries provide explanations and historical facts surrounding particular verses in Scripture. One of the reasons I like the *NIV Life Application Study Bible* so much is that the commentary is right in the Bible near the related text. If your Bible doesn't have such commentary, check your local Christian bookstore for many fine stand-alone commentary options; some reliable commentaries can even be found online. Or ask someone from your church's pastoral staff to advise you on which commentaries are acceptable within your denomination. I suspect this will be a question they will be delighted to answer!

If you don't have any access to additional resources to help you understand certain passages, you might do two things. First, ask God to clearly reveal the truth you are supposed to understand from the Scripture you are reading. And, second, make sure you read the sections of Scripture before and after a particular verse to ensure you gain greater insight into the writer's intention. Some verses can take on completely different meanings than intended if you pluck them out of their context.

After reading several blurbs of commentary within my Bible, I discover that before Paul was a believer, he was a Jewish religious leader who persecuted, imprisoned, and killed Christians for their faith. Then he had a dramatic, life-changing encounter with Jesus and was never the same — transformed into a passionate follower of Christ and a missionary called especially to reach non-Jewish people called Gentiles. Wow. Talk about someone who discovered God in a major way. Paul obviously was a man who understood how to get beyond church just being a routine and into living every day totally sold out to God. This is a man I want to hear from.

Paul had visited the Ephesians during one of his missionary trips and stayed with them almost three years. His letter to them is full of great love and affection because he knew these people so well.

Now that I know the context of these verses and who wrote them, I can look at any given passage from the book and better understand how it fits within Ephesians as a whole.

READ THE PASSAGE PHRASE BY PHRASE

Because every word and phrase within the Bible has been intentionally and divinely placed, much discovery and revelation awaits us whenever we study.

To do this, write down the words of your verse on a piece of paper, then underline the individual words or word phrases that seem to work together. Once you've done so, ponder why these words or phrases are in this particular passage and what value they add to it. It's a great journaling exercise.

Watch what happens when we follow this process with Ephesians 1:17: "I keep asking that the God of our Lord Jesus Christ, the glorious Father, may give you the Spirit of wisdom and revelation, so that you may know him better."

"I keep asking ..." Notice Paul doesn't pray just once that the Ephesians would have wisdom and revelation; he keeps asking. In other words, this is a constant prayer. His example challenges me to make it a habit to keep asking God for wisdom and revelation. In doing so, I admit my daily dependence on God and my need for Him. This keeps me humble by reminding me that all wisdom and revelation are gifts

from God, not something I can conjure up on my own because I am so clever or smart.

Keep asking. This statement is rich with discipline and perseverance and determination. This must have been how Paul himself prayed. His transformation from a persecutor of Christians to a servant of Christ was immediate and astonishing. The Bible says, "At once he began to preach in the synagogues that Jesus is the Son of God. All those who heard him were astonished" (Acts 9:20–21). How could he so quickly know enough about Jesus to go from killing Christians to preaching the gospel?

If this kind of astonishing wisdom and revelation was available to Paul, who just days before lived as an enemy to Christ and His followers, I have to believe the same can be true for us.

Keep asking.

"the God of our Lord Jesus Christ, the glorious Father ..." Isn't it amazing that we can go to God personally and ask Him for things and about things? We can unashamedly sit, swinging our Keds back and forth, and talk as honestly with the Creator of the universe as I did with the preacher man. Only God won't get red-faced and offended. He doesn't have root issues and triggers like people do. He is a "glorious Father."

Glorious can mean several things, but my two favorite definitions are: "entitled to great renown" and "completely enjoyable."[2]

What a beautiful way to think of God. We aren't asking a remote, distant, angry, rule-thumping, finger-wagging deity. We are asking God, the God of our Lord Jesus. Our glorious Father who is entitled to the utmost renown and yet at the same time is completely enjoyable.

"may give you the Spirit of wisdom and revelation ..." Again, note the interesting word choice here. Instead of praying the Ephesians will have wisdom and revelation, Paul asks God to give them the *Spirit* of wisdom and revelation. Why might this be?

Just asking for wisdom and revelation is but scratching the surface of what Paul wants for the Ephesians. Having wisdom and revelation might help them make a good choice or two, but Paul wants them to have the *Spirit* of wisdom and revelation so that their every word, every attitude, every action and reaction, every thought is infused with the wisdom of God and reined in by His revelation.

Oh yes, that is what I want for sure! I don't just want to be a woman who has wisdom and revelation; I want to be a woman who has the *Spirit* of wisdom and revelation working around me, in me, through me, ahead of me—especially when those raging hormones threaten my best intentions. Amen, sister. Now there is a sermon that will preach!

"so that you may know him better." The "so that" part of this verse reveals the intentions of the heart. We ask and keep asking for wisdom and revelation for one reason alone: to know our Lord better.

I don't ask for this type of wisdom "so that" I can make better business decisions. Or "so that" I can manipulate my circumstances. Or "so that" I can jockey for a better position with more power and prestige. Or "so that" I can feel smart when I throw out the perfect answer at next week's Bible study.

No. It really has nothing to do with me at all. Having the Spirit of wisdom and revelation is purely "so that" I can know God better. Really know Him. Not just know facts about Him. But know Him in even deeper ways than I ever thought possible.

Having the Spirit of wisdom and revelation is purely "so that" I can know God better. Really know Him.

This is my greatest desire. The one planted in me as a little girl when I caught a glimpse that it was possible for me to learn about God, talk with Him, and apply His teachings in a way that makes a difference in the way I live.

DO TRY THIS AT HOME

Now it's your turn to give it a try. In your journal or on the next page, take the next two verses in the Ephesians 1 passage we've been looking at together and practice the phrase-by-phrase Bible study exercise yourself. Don't fret. Great treasures of wisdom, revelation, growth, and connection with God await you. You'll become a self-feeder, a woman who can dig into God's Word in order to let it rearrange you so you know God more deeply.

My girlhood meeting with the preacher man didn't work out so well. But my daily meetings with God are glorious and completely enjoyable. I pray yours will be as well.

And please pray for me. My mother always took great delight in hoping I would have kids just like me. He answered her prayers five times over. Have mercy!

EPHESIANS 1:17 – 19

[17]I keep asking that the God of our Lord Jesus Christ, the glorious Father, may give you the Spirit of wisdom and revelation, so that you may know him better. [18]I pray also that the eyes of your heart may be enlightened in order that you may know the hope to which he has called you, the riches of his glorious inheritance in the saints, [19]and his incomparably great power for us who believe.

Chapter 5

DEVOTION TIME BLUES

My husband half whispered and half chuckled to my friend Holly, "I think Lysa's a little premenstrual." He meant premenopausal, but his slip made me laugh even though I *was* having one of *those* days and in no laughing mood. In reality, I was having one of *those* weeks. And it had nothing to do with any hormonal imbalance.

I had let my frustration level mount to the point where every little thing bothered me. On a scale from one to ten, my emotions hovered at about 8.5. And then when anything happened, I'd boil over time and time again.

It was a week jam-packed with deadlines, appointments for the kids, and getting ready for my sister and her family's visit. Since we live seven hours apart, she rarely gets to come to my house. Call it hospitality or pride issues, I just wanted everything to look nice. You know: clean, tidy, welcoming, slightly better than one of our average at-home days.

I wanted to prove that I'd long since outgrown those nasty teenager housekeeping habits I was famous for when we both still lived at home; that I'd matured just a tad. After all, I was fairly certain she'd be reporting back to our mama after our weekend together. I wasn't going overboard, but I figured she'd like to sleep in sheets free of dog hair and walk on floors to which her feet didn't stick.

All was going well until my kids decided to be kids. Let's just say the outcome has ensured that I will never land a feature spread for our home in *Southern Living* magazine. Not that having my home sandwiched between articles about food I can't cook and vacations we can't afford has ever been a goal; I'm just stating a fact.

The whole getting-ready-for-my-sister-coming had intensified my "mama statements," things I say to my kids over and over all the time but I especially wanted them to get right that particular weekend. Things like:

- We flush every time we go in this house — no exceptions.
- An empty toilet paper roll is a call to action before you sit down, people.
- The dryer lint must be cleaned out after every load lest you want our house to burn down and render us homeless.
- If the orange juice container is empty, it goes in the trash — not back in the fridge.
- When Mom says we are eating leftovers, it does not translate into asking your brother to drive you to Target so you can eat candy and pretzels instead.
- We'd all be much happier if toenails were clipped outside and not at the kitchen table — hello sanitation violation.
- If you spill something sweet and sticky on the floor, just humor me and clean it before the ants descend.

It just never crossed my mind that I would ever need to add to the list: "If you find a mattress in the neighbor's trash pile, do not place it in our pond and use it as a flotation device. Because then it will fill up with water and be impossible to get out of the pond. And then everyone who comes to visit will suddenly have a flashback to a certain Jeff Foxworthy comedy skit called, 'You might be a redneck if . . . you have a dadgum mattress floating in the pond in your front yard.'"

Right when it happened, my husband told the kids to take care of said mattress situation. And they did. They went out and jumped and jumped and jumped until the mattress sank. Of course, they didn't tell us that's how they'd taken care of it. We just assumed it was back in the trash pile.

And then one beautiful morning as the sun rose, so did the mattress. Only now, the urgency of the situation hit DEFCON 1 level as it suddenly occurred to me that the mattress would in fact be the very first thing my sister and her family noticed as they approached our house.

A floating mattress. And we're not talking about an air mattress that might be mistaken for a float. No, we are talking go-lift-up-your-covers-and-look-at-that-thing-you-sleep-on-every-night. Yeah, the one with the springs and the padding. Now floating in my pond. Complete with turtles sunning on the top for added effect.

The mattress was, in fact, the first thing my sister noticed as she turned in the driveway. And I'm sad to say that I was so frustrated about things not being up to the standard I'd hoped for that I couldn't even see the humor in the situation.

Normally, I would have. But it had been a week in which everything else had crowded out my time with the Lord, and it took quite a toll on my peace of mind. The longer I went without meeting with God, the more desperate, cloudy, and starved my soul became.

Running on empty eventually causes things to break down and stall out. That's quite honestly where I was. As if my life wasn't already sounding like a bad country song, now I was also singing the devotion time blues.

WHY IS HAVING A QUIET TIME WITH JESUS SO IMPORTANT?

When Jesus rose from the grave and appeared in the midst of His disciples meeting behind locked doors, I imagine they were stunned, shocked, and overjoyed. With great intentionality, Jesus chose the words He used to greet them. Of all the themes He could have selected at that moment, He picked what they needed most. What was it?

Joy?

Hope?

Love?

While all of these certainly would have been appropriate, Jesus didn't touch on any of them. He simply said over and over again, "Peace be with you!" According to John 20, it is the first thing He said. He said it again before breathing on them to receive the Holy Spirit. Then when addressing Thomas and his doubts, He said it again, "Peace be with you!"

And isn't it interesting that each time Jesus is recorded as saying this, the writer ends the sentence with an exclamation point. This tells me that not only was Jesus intentional, He was also emphatic. His words were conveyed with great emphasis and urgency.

Why peace?

And why did Jesus use the particular phrasing, "Peace be with you!"?

I have a theory. This world is very good at conjuring up facades. Temporary moments of worldly happiness can appear joyful. The world takes hope and mistakes it for wishful thinking. And the world has made "love" a dime-store word used to describe a feeling that can change with the wind.

The world's offering of joy, hope, and love is fleeting, temporary, and dangerously unstable ... but it can put on a good show in the short term.

"I got that promotion — joy!"

"I think we can afford this house — hope!"

"He likes spending time with me — I think I'm in love!"

However, jobs can be lost in an instant, houses can be foreclosed on, and feelings of love go as quickly as they come.

The world's offering of joy, hope, and love is fleeting, temporary, and dangerously unstable ... but it can put on a good show in the short term.

So, really, what the world offers — for a moment or two — is false joy, false hope, and false love.

But it cannot offer false peace. It can offer peaceful settings and rituals to conjure up peaceful thoughts … but not true soul contentedness. The peace that flows despite circumstances can only be found through Jesus being with us. That's why Jesus phrased it the way He did, "Peace be with you!" In other words, "You can walk through anything, My sweet follower, if you realize that I am peace and I am with you."

Why is it so important to spend time with Jesus every day? Because He will give us the exact instruction and comfort we need to handle all He sees coming our way — how to act and, even more challenging, how to react in every situation. It is the perfect measure of His peace, packaged up just for us. With great expectation, we can stick it in our pocket and carry it with us. Instead of being slaves to our emotions and reacting based on our feelings, we can remain victoriously peaceful no matter what.

A few months ago we had dinner with a couple who were asking lots of questions about how Art and I handle all that we have on our plates — five kids, a growing ministry, a restaurant business. We assured them that some days we handle everything well but, honestly, other days get a little wacky.

Then the husband paused and said, "Yes, but through it all you just seem to have such peace."

And with that I smiled.

He was right. At least partially, anyhow. When I take the time to meet with Jesus each morning, I am prepared to face life with much more peace than if I just rush into my day without Him.

Because God is able to stand in my yesterday, today, and tomorrow, He knows things and sees things for which I need to be prepared. I love how the psalmist expresses this truth: "O LORD, you have searched me and you know me. You know when I sit and when I rise; you perceive my thoughts from afar. You discern my going out and my lying down; you are familiar with all my ways. Before a word is even on my tongue you know it completely, O LORD" (Psalm 139:1 – 4). The Lord perceives the thoughts we'll think and the words we'll speak in response, and He wants to prepare us, interrupt us, and maybe even rearrange us. He loves us enough to desire to protect us from our natural-flesh responses.

If you're anything like me, maybe you find yourself quite often crying out, "God, help me." If I've spent time with Jesus that morning, it's amazing how what He taught me hours before comes flooding back in that desperate moment — and it is exactly what I need. If my heart has been prepared to receive God's most perfect help, I am able to receive it right when I need it and I'm much more likely to apply it immediately.

It seems like such an elementary thing to state that we should spend time with Jesus and read the Bible every day. Of course we should. We know this. It's one of the first things we learn in Christianity 101. But it's amazing how I'll sit down to do this and suddenly a million urgent action items flood my brain. Suddenly it's so tempting to answer an email, throw in a load of laundry, write out a grocery list, and start getting my day in order.

However, if I fail to get my heart in order first, I am guaranteeing myself a misplaced attitude that day. Hands down. Without exception. If I don't spend time with Jesus, my reactions will be harsher, my perspectives a little more self-centered, my emotions a little more on edge, and my tongue a little less grace-filled.

IS IT OKAY TO STRUGGLE?

Have you ever been at a church service when the teacher asked everyone to turn to a particular book of the Bible and you couldn't for the life of you remember where in the Bible that book is located? And for Pete's sake, have you noticed how loud Bible pages are?

You start to sweat while everyone else around you opens their Bibles right to that passage. You feel every eye is suddenly on you and your noisy Bible pages. Heaven forbid you actually turn to the table of contents to get a page number. You sink under the enormous weight of perceived judgmental glances.

The reality is, some of those who so easily turned to that Scripture are just sitting there with their Bibles cracked open to the wrong place pretending to be following along. And, with any luck, the others are too engaged in God's Word to notice. So relax, sister, turn to the table of contents and realize there is no shame in doing so!

There is also no shame in admitting to God you are struggling in your devotional time with Him. You are not alone. When I surveyed women on my blog about their devotional times, their comments overwhelmingly confirm that this is an area in which many of us want to improve but often don't know how. Listen to a few:

> **Anonymous:** Do I ever struggle with my quiet time? Yes, yes, yes. I have been a born-again Christian for the past thirteen years. I would love to say that I have accomplished a quiet time with God each day. That just is not the case.

> **Kelli:** Yes, I can definitely struggle with feeling the duty of devotion rather than the desire, but I still feel that it's so important to spend that time with God daily. Sometimes the emotions are just not there, but we still need to obey and do it. I do not always feel giddy in love with my husband, but I commit to loving him and acting respectfully. Same goes with kids, and so many other things in life. It's not about the feelings, but about making the decision to love.

> **Carol:** I think we've all struggled with having a quiet time at some point or another. Just like the ups and downs in our lives, we have ups and downs in our times with the Lord. During the down times, I sometimes do feel like it is a duty.

There is no shame in admitting to God you are struggling in your devotional time with Him. You are not alone.

Women confessed that they felt ill-equipped and intimidated to study God's Word on their own. Even more alarming, women admitted that they see their time with God as a mundane thing they do out of habit rather than as a way that God will speak to them, help them, and equip them for a more meaningful life.

So how do we go about getting jump-started in this area? When I first started having daily devotions, I always brought a devotional book, my Bible, and a journal to my quiet time. I read a reading or chapter of the book and looked up any verses that corresponded with it. If the Lord was really speaking that day, I would journal as well. As time passed, I finished the books and found I didn't need them as much to have a good quiet time because I craved His Word instead. Right now, I read from one to three chapters of whatever book of the Bible I'm studying and highlight verses that really speak to me. Sometimes I even write a verse or two on a 3 x 5 card and carry it with me throughout the day.

Oh, how we underestimate the power made available to us when we spend time with God. Our earthly eyes are so limited because they don't allow us to see what is happening in the heavenly realm. A daily battle is being fought for our attention and our devotion. Satan would love nothing more than to keep us separated from the power God gives us during our time with Him. It's time to stop feeling guilty and ill-equipped and start embracing the incredible privilege to meet with Jesus every day.

Remember, devotions don't have to be perfect to be powerful and effective. Jesus just wants a willing soul to come to Him — to verbalize her desire to seek Him and acknowledge her need for Him. Then He'll show you how to make your devotions exactly what you need.

PRACTICALLY SPEAKING, HOW DO I DO THIS?

Remember my mattress situation from the beginning of this chapter? Well, I knew I needed God to change my perspective on the whole situation. So, before my Bible study the next day, I asked God to lead me to the perfect Scripture to study. Most days before I start my time with the Lord, I pray that very simple prayer I mentioned in chapter one that ushers my heart into the right place with God:

God, I want to see You. God, I want to hear You. God, I want to know You. So that I can follow hard after You.

This prayer is not a magic formula, just four short sentences that perfectly express my desire to really experience God throughout my day. I want to see Him working in me, around me, and through me. I want to hear His voice so clearly that I won't doubt when He asks for my obedience. I want to know Him — not just facts about Him — but really know Him personally and intimately. And lastly, I want to follow hard after Him, to be the woman He wants me to be in every circumstance of my day.

It's amazing that when I verbalize my heart's desire in this way, something inside of me shifts and I'm ready for the Word of God in a fresh way. I don't want to just read and pray to check it off my to-do list. I see this time, instead, as preparation for the great adventure God and I are about to head off on together in the hours ahead. Talk about shifting the way to look at your quiet time! Talk about going from feeling dry and tired to being fired up and inspired!

I found myself in the middle of the mattress situation wanting desperately for God to rearrange my outlook. This just felt like such a meaningless pain in the neck. (Ever been there?)

I asked the Lord to come to me quickly and interrupt my natural-flesh response before I blew some sort of gasket. I don't even know what a gasket is, but I'm fairly certain it ain't pretty when one blows.

I choked out a very simple prayer, *Encourage me, Lord, please.*

As I opened the Bible, I turned to the book of Psalms. This is a great place to start when we feel a need to pour out our most honest feelings to God. I flipped through a few pages before I finally landed on a treasure of a verse: "Teach me your way, O LORD, and I will walk in your truth; give me an undivided heart, that I may fear your name" (Psalm 86:11).

I continued my prayer. *Lord, thank You for this verse. Yes, I want an undivided heart. I love that part of this verse. My heart can get so divided and stretched and pulled in a million directions. Thank You for this reminder. Also, could You send something else my way today that would just be a practical bit of encouragement? I could really use that as well.*

The minute I finished praying, my eyes fell on the first part of the verse. "Teach me your way, O LORD, and I will walk in your truth." I had been so excited about the undivided heart part of the verse that I'd brushed right past the first part.

The phrase "teach me your way" wouldn't leave me. Those four words just kept running through my mind. Kind of like when you get a song stuck in your head and, like it or not, you're singing it, humming it, and tapping your fingers to it all day long.

Eventually, I came to realize that these words were the encouragement God was giving me in response to my request.

I wanted to be appreciative but, to be honest, I'd had something else in mind. I don't know, like maybe getting a call from a gal you might have heard of named Beth who teaches Bible studies saying she'd like to go out for coffee. Or maybe a guy named Ty suddenly showing up on my front doorstep offering to foot the bill for an extreme home makeover. You know, nothing terribly huge.

Instead, I'd be sipping up my grande latte with four words, "Teach me your way."

I pulled my Bible back out and reread the verse in context just to see if I could understand what God was trying to teach me. Finally, I saw something besides just four words.

There are many ways I can choose to react when things happen each day. I can choose the way of "It's my right to be frustrated." I can choose the way of "Doesn't anyone listen to me around here?" I can choose the way of "Do you know how this makes me feel?"

Or, I can choose to let God teach me His way.

My way leads to all kinds of runaway feelings that pull me away from the truth and into an absolute pit of yuck.

His way leads to calmly finding a solution without all the anger and frustration. His way leads to me being able to extend grace—the same grace I so desperately need myself. And His way leads me to the truth.

The truth is, it's a bummer when you have a mattress as a front yard ornament. And it's a bummer that said situation couldn't be fixed in time for my sister's visit. But why compound those bummers and make them even worse by adding runaway emotions?

I can honestly say, learning more about His way and walking in His truth despite my feelings was a great gift of encouragement. I couldn't believe how His truth coursing through my body calmed my racing pulse. And I was even more encouraged because I didn't have to deal with the yuck that comes after losing my cool. God is good.

I later found myself laughing with a friend over this whole situation. She asked me if I had considered putting the story in this book. I told her no ... there might be too many chapters that started off with some kind of everyday life antic that put me on the edge of a breakdown only to have Jesus talk me off the coffee table and teach me something new in the process.

She laughed back. "Lysa, isn't that where most of us live? And isn't that sort of the point of your book?"

Why, yes it is. Applying God's truths to everything in my life has moved me past singing the devotion time blues and onto some really hip-and-happening praise music despite my rock-and-roll circumstances.

Are you ready to deepen your connection with God? Remember, we aren't after perfectly accomplishing our quiet time routine. Mercy, don't we already have too many things pulling at us? No, I'm talking about seeing our time with God as the most precious and valuable minutes of our day.

So, start small if you need to. Just five or ten minutes. Or if you already set this time aside each day but it feels empty and lacking in the power I've described, spend the next few days praying to God for a renewal of vision for your time with Him. Ask Him for the power. Confess your lack of motivation and struggles with distraction.

And for those of you who are really doing well in this area right now, will you spend some time praying for those of us who are struggling?

Oh sweet friends, my greatest desire would be to lead you into a more meaningful, life-changing, perspective-rearranging relationship with Jesus. If this chapter has at all accomplished that, my prayers for this book have been answered!

Chapter 6

UNLIKELY LESSONS
FROM A PINEAPPLE

I have a love-hate relationship with all things culinary. Remember the tragic end of my great adventure in selling kitchen gadgets? Yes, I agree, let's not remember that.

The thing is, I am a creative person and I love to eat. So, one would think the kitchen would be the perfect place for me. However, there is just too much pressure. I like for the creative mood to strike me every couple of days or so. But the people I live with like to eat three meals ... *a day*.

And then there is this issue with the shelf life of fresh food. I can go to the store, buy all kinds of breads and fresh meats and green things, but by the time I get everything put away I have used up all my brain cells. Once I remotivate myself to do something with all those supplies, half of them have gone bad. Then I feel terrible and resort to boxed items, the just-add-water kind.

You know it's bad when your lack of kitchen savvy starts to affect the way your kids think about cooking. The other day my nine-year-old daughter was pretending she was the next Rachael Ray as she demonstrated to her pretend TV audience how to make sweet rolls.

She first instructed her audience to lay out all the ingredients, preheat the oven, and melt some butter in the microwave. Then she took a triangle of crescent roll dough from a tube and told her audience to butter one side and sprinkle it with cinnamon sugar. "Then you take a marshmallow and hold it up. You check all sides of it make sure there is no mold. Then you wrap the crescent roll around it."

Excuse me? Did my child just instruct the pretend thousands watching her show that the marshmallows from my kitchen must be checked for *mold*?

Now, lest you think I am totally inept in the kitchen, I've mastered a few dishes of which I am exceedingly proud. Not proud as in bragging. But proud as in relieved to have some evidence that I can wield a kitchen utensil or two and actually produce positive results. This will be my proof if one of my kids brings up the whole molding-marshmallows thing on a therapist's couch one day.

Take, for instance, the pineapple. I love fresh-cut pineapple. I love the way it tastes. I love that it has no fat grams. And I love that it can be served at any meal—breakfast, lunch, or dinner—as the perfect, healthy side dish.

The problem with fresh pineapples is that they are slightly complicated in their original form. To hold up a fresh pineapple and look upon it longingly can be quite frustrating when you haven't a clue how to properly cut it open. So, for years I would walk by the fresh pineapples in the grocery store produce section, heave a sigh, and head straight to the aisle where the fruits and veggies of the less-fresh variety were shelved. The canned version was fine in a pinch but honestly didn't compare to the fresh. It simply teased my taste buds that greater possibilities existed.

Then one day a friend I was visiting asked me if I'd like a snack. I gasped when she brought out a real pineapple. With ease she turned the fruit on its side and chopped off the top and the bottom. Then she sat it upright on its level end and proceeded to cut sections from each side, starting at the edge of the core. She then shaved off the outer skin, chopped the fruit into bite-sized pieces, and handed me a whole bowlful.

I was amazed. That's it? That's all there is to it? You mean for years I've missed out on the goodness of fresh pineapples because I couldn't figure out how to do *that*?

I drove directly to the grocery store, confidently marched up to the produce section, and grabbed a pineapple of my very own. I wanted to chat it up with the others there in the produce section. "Do you see what I have in my cart? That's right, a fresh pineapple. Yup, I just love cutting up these wild fruits, don't you?" The empowerment of just a little know-how can sure work wonders.

THE PINEAPPLE PRINCIPLE

For years, I took the same approach with studying the Bible as I did with the pineapple. I looked at biblical truth from afar. I didn't feel equipped to open it and attempt to study it on my own. Instead of reading the fresh truth for myself, I only read books that talked *about* the Bible. Just like that canned pineapple, my experience with learning God's truth teased me that greater possibilities existed. But since I had no idea how to get them for myself, I avoided the Bible and settled for whatever I could glean from other people.

That is, until I attended a Bible study in which the teacher modeled how to open up the Bible and study it for ourselves. Each week I watched her dig into Scriptures with a passion and hunger for truth that I'd never known. The way she put verses into context and brought out the meanings from the original text amazed me. Slowly, I decided to try it for myself.

Much of what I learned in opening up the Bible for myself I've already mentioned in the previous two chapters. We've discussed the importance of finding out how to know the author and context of books within the Bible, and how to break verses apart to unearth their rich meanings. We've also learned about the process by which we can discover God's provision for us through daily devotion times. Now I want to focus more closely on life application.

After all, don't we get into God's Word so it can get into us? So that it can interrupt us, change us, satisfy us? How sad to simply settle for learning facts about the Bible when it was meant for so much more.

Becoming more than a good Bible study girl means pursuing God's truth so passionately that it actually becomes part of our nature. The apostle James writes, "Therefore, get rid of all moral filth and the evil that is so prevalent and humbly accept the word planted in you, which can save you. Do not merely listen to the word, and so deceive yourselves. Do what it says" (James 1:21 – 22).

The more we make a habit of applying God's Word to our lives, the more it becomes part of our nature, our natural way of acting and reacting. Knowing God's Word and doing what it says not only saves us from heartbreak and trouble, it also brings more satisfaction to our souls than anything else ever could. Think about that for just a minute. Aren't security and satisfaction what many people spend their every waking minute pursuing? Yet, the world's answers are temporary facades that disappoint every time. Not just sometimes, every time.

The only time-tested, foolproof instruction for how to get our basic soul needs met is found in the Bible. But it's a two-part process. We must not only read and study the Bible but also develop the habit of living out its message in our everyday lives. If people ever say that Jesus and His biblical truths don't work, I am quick to ask how consistently they've applied what they've read. People fail; truth never does.

One of the most exciting ways to move Bible study from theory to real-life application is by looking closely at the life stories of the men and women who walked its pages. So, let's pick a Bible character who

---

If people ever say that Jesus and His biblical truths don't work, I am quick to ask how consistently they've applied what they've read. People fail; truth never does.

---

successfully lived out truth, see the difference it made in his life, and how we can be inspired to live the same.

DAVID AND GOLIATH: THE BACK STORY

The story of David and Goliath has been the pride and joy of Sunday school flannel boards for years. It's your basic little-guy-versus-big-guy tale, with impossible odds and a glorious victory for the deserving underdog.

If you grew up in Sunday school or know the gist of the account, you may be tempted to breeze right past it. However, wrapped in this familiar story are some often-overlooked but significant details that are worth slowing down for. Unearthing these details has profoundly changed the way I look at the ordinary tasks I set about doing on my many ordinary days.

To best understand how David's story unfolds in 1 Samuel 17, it's a good idea to back up and read chapter 16 first. There we learn that King Saul had displeased God—he had been obedient, but only to a certain point. In fact, Saul was much more concerned with pleasing people than he was with pleasing God. As a result, God eventually revealed to the prophet Samuel that a new king should be anointed to take Saul's place.

God also revealed to Samuel that the future king of Israel would come from the house of Jesse, so Samuel sent word to Jesse to call together all of his sons. When they arrived, Samuel immediately focused on Jesse's oldest, a fine-looking young man. He probably looked like a king, smelled like a king, and, being the eldest, he was positioned like a king. But the Lord told Samuel, "Do not consider his outward appearance or his height, for I have rejected him. The LORD does not look at the things man looks at. Man looks at the outward appearance, but the LORD looks at the heart" (1 Samuel 16:7). Now, this verse in and of itself could preach to me for days and cause me to do some serious character inspection within my own heart. I could look up the word "heart" at biblegateway.com[3] and spend time reading through many verses regarding the importance of guarding my heart and allowing only God to reign there.

This is the beautiful thing about studying a story while at the same time examining our own character. Allowing the traits of biblical characters to cause us to do some introspective thinking will deepen our study and make what we're learning more applicable to our lives.

God obviously takes the spiritual condition of the heart very seriously. It was the requirement of utmost importance when God was looking to pick a future king. And since God doesn't change, we can discern that the condition of a person's heart is still a top priority of His today.

Have you been longing for something to happen in your life for a long time? Have you ever asked the question, "God, what do You require of me?" The answer to a question like this has everything to do with our character needing to be developed to match our calling.

In our story, Samuel passed over all of the sons Jesse paraded before him. None were chosen to be the future king. Samuel then asked Jesse if he had any other sons. Jesse responded, "There is still the youngest, but he is tending the sheep" (1 Samuel 16:11).

Isn't it strange that Jesse didn't bring forward all of his sons in the first place? He was instructed to bring them *all* before Samuel, but for some reason he didn't even consider David. Again, park here for a minute. Anytime something seems out of order or not quite normal in Scripture, it's wise to pause and ask *why*? Some of my greatest spiritual insights have come from doing this.

Why wouldn't David have been included? Surely it wasn't merely for logistical reasons. There must have been some servant who could have temporarily watched over David's sheep. I mean, think of the magnitude of this opportunity! Imagine if Congress called you today and informed you that the next president of the United States was going to be chosen from among your kids. You'd have them excused from soccer practice. You'd tell them to find a coworker to cover their shift at their after-school job. You'd let them miss the afternoon tutoring session for that underwater basket-weaving class. Nothing would keep you from making sure that they were all spiffed up, lined up, and ready for inspection.

That David was not even brought before Samuel gives us crucial evidence about David's position in his family. He was overlooked by everyone. Overlooked by everyone, but handpicked by God. Again, this could be another whole study in itself. Just understanding this one fact about David could positively change a person's outlook on life. How many of us have let the entire scope of how God could use us in life be tainted by the hurt of being overlooked by others?

Being overlooked and rejected by people does not equate to being overlooked and rejected by God. Often it means exactly the opposite. Consider these words from the apostle Paul: "That is why, for Christ's sake, I delight in weaknesses, in insults, in hardships, in persecutions, in difficulties. For when I am weak, then I am strong" (2 Corinthians 12:10). David's story is a beautiful illustration of this truth. This encourages me when I feel weak, insulted, faced with hardships, persecuted, or in a difficult place. For the sake of Christ, I can delight in the fact that the things that make me feel weak only serve to make me a stronger, more capable person.

Being overlooked and rejected by people does not equate to being overlooked and rejected by God. Often it means exactly the opposite.

As soon as David was brought in from the fields, God confirmed to Samuel that David would be the future king. He didn't look like a king, he wasn't positioned like a king, and he certainly didn't smell like a king, but something about his heart made David the chosen one.

Once he was anointed, "the Spirit of the LORD came upon David in power" (1 Samuel 16:13). God picked David, and He would strengthen and train him as well.

Where did God choose for the training to take place? Surely David would be sent to Israel's most exclusive training center. Maybe the Jerusalem campus of Harvard? Or a Sinai leadership academy? Maybe a crash course in political science and national defense strategy? As I was reading the text, I couldn't wait to see where David would be sent next.

I admit I was slightly disappointed to learn that David was sent back into the fields to tend his sheep. David still had the oil of a king's anointing dripping from his forehead, yet we find him in the common fields of everyday life. Might David be wondering, *I thought I was chosen to lead people, not sheep? I thought I was headed to a golden throne, but here I am laying down in green pastures.*

It is tough to be in a place of waiting. Waiting can sometimes consume a person with questions, wants, and worries. Though David has been told he'll be the next king, God doesn't allow him to take his rightful throne just yet. So I can imagine the temptation was there to question God's timing, to want God to hurry things up a bit, and to worry that somehow God had forgotten him.

Questions, wants, and worries are all things I deal with when I find myself in a time of waiting. Learning how David dealt with his waiting period helps me to have a more patient perspective in my own times of waiting.

In David's story, I see that God's waiting period serves an incredible purpose, not the least of which is David's preparation. And nothing in Scripture, here in 1 Samuel or elsewhere, indicates that David was at all bothered by the delay.

As a matter of fact, one of the most beloved of David's psalms, Psalm 23, begins: "The LORD is my shepherd, I shall not be in want." Although scholars debate about when David wrote Psalm 23 — when he was young or when he was old—I think it provides a beautiful snapshot of what his perspective may have been during this time of waiting.

He didn't wonder or resist why God had put him in this most unlikely place for an anointed king. He didn't let his mind be carried off by doubt and insecurity. He just accepted that God had led him where he was supposed to be—the right place for right now. Whew, this is hard for me sometimes! I find myself wanting to rush things, to get past the waiting as quickly as possible. Sometimes I forget that God is doing significant things around me and in me, even while I am waiting. Good thing I'm doing this character study to be reminded of this!

Although David might have written Psalm 23 from an experience of questioning, wanting, or worrying, he recognized the Lord as his shepherd. Just as David would have always had the best interests of his sheep in mind, he trusted God in this same way. Then he expressed his understanding of God's purpose for his waiting period when he wrote, "He makes me lie down in green pastures [rest], he leads me beside quiet waters [reflection], he restores my soul [restoration]. He guides me in paths of righteousness [right choices] for his name's sake [it is all about God, not about David]" (Psalm 23:2–3).

David chose to resist the temptation of discontentment by seeing the greater good of this waiting period. Rest, reflection, restoration, learning to make right choices, and remembering it is all about God and not me are all positive ways to spend any nervous energy that might come my way during my own next waiting period.

DAVID AND GOLIATH: THE GIANT FALLS

In addition to tending his sheep, David's preparation also included serving the king and his father, Jesse. When King Saul felt anxious and tormented, the only thing that comforted him was David's soothing music. David served his father by running errands—delivering food and messages to his brothers on the battlefield.

Wait a minute, David's training sure does sound a whole lot like my everyday life: tending, serving, running errands. Suddenly, David's story hits very close to home. I'll admit I've struggled at times feeling a lack of purpose in my tending, serving, and running errands. I love my family, but the long to-do lists that come with managing a family can leave a girl feeling a little used up and worn out. But if I can see a greater good being worked out in me through these to-do items, they take on new meaning. Just as with David, God can use the tasks of my everyday life to develop my character to the point that it matches my calling. And that just puts a whole new spin on all that tending and serving and running around, doesn't it?

One of David's errands took him to the front lines of the battle-field to deliver wine and bread to his brothers. Only there wasn't much battle happening. With the Israelites encamped on one hill and their enemies, the Philistines, encamped across a valley on another hill, everything had come to a standstill. Neither army wanted to be the first to rush down into the valley to try to take their opponent's hill. That was a first-class ticket to a bloodbath.

The Philistines devised an alternate plan. They sent Goliath, their biggest, mightiest warrior, into the valley to insult the Israelites and challenge their best warrior to fight him one-on-one: whoever won the battle would declare victory for their entire army. But when the Israelites saw the size of Goliath, they were terrified, and no one dared to accept his challenge.

No one, that is, until David caught wind of the news. David asked, "Who is this uncircumcised Philistine that he should defy the armies of the living God?" (1 Samuel 17:26). His brothers initially made fun of him for asking, but word soon got around the Israelite camp that a man among them was willing to face Goliath. When word reached King Saul, he sent for this man to be brought to his tent.

Imagine Saul's great disappointment when he saw the simple shepherd boy whose gentle music had soothed him. He immediately expressed doubts about David's abilities, but David established his qualifications by referring back to the training he had in the fields of everyday life:

> But David said to Saul, "Your servant has been keeping his father's sheep. When a lion or a bear came and carried off a sheep from the flock, I went after it, struck it and rescued the sheep from its mouth. When it turned on me, I seized it by its hair, struck it and killed it. Your servant has killed both the lion and the bear; this uncircumcised Philistine will be like one of them, because he has defied the armies of the living God. The LORD who delivered me from the paw of the lion and the paw of the bear will deliver me from the hand of this Philistine."
>
> Saul said to David, "Go, and the LORD be with you." (1 Samuel 17:34–37)

Indeed, it was in the fields of everyday life that David's character was developed to match his calling. All that tending and serving and errand-running was not a waste of time; in fact, it was the best use of time. It's where David gained the courage that would soon be required of him to defeat Goliath.

With nothing but a simple sling and five stones, David faced the giant. Only he was no longer an overlooked shepherd boy but an anointed king operating in God's power.

> David said to the Philistine, "You come against me with sword and spear and javelin, but I come against you in the name of the LORD Almighty, the God of the armies of Israel, whom you have defied. This day the LORD will hand you over to me, and I'll strike you down and cut off your head. Today I will give the carcasses of the Philistine army to the birds of the air and the beasts of the earth, and the whole world will know that there is a God in Israel. All those gathered here will know that it is not by sword

or spear that the LORD saves; for the battle is the LORD's, and he will give all of you into our hands." (1 Samuel 17:45–47)

The passage goes on to describe how David then ran quickly toward the giant. And I can't help but think the words that would one day become Psalm 23 were once again coursing through David's mind, "Even though I walk through the valley of the shadow of death, I will fear no evil, for you are with me" (Psalm 23:4).

Amazing. I've read Psalm 23 many times but never thought of it as it might have applied to this story. David was in a valley. A giant would certainly have cast quite a shadow. And though David should have been afraid, knowing that God was with him made him absolutely fearless as he ran straight to the center of God's will.

The climax of this story is just too good for me paraphrase, so it's time for you to take it from here. Why not turn to 1 Samuel 17:48 and keep on going?

Can you believe all that we've already learned from studying part of David's story? Better yet, can you believe all the many ways our character could be improved by applying the principles from David's story to our own lives? And remember, there are many, many other Bible characters with whom you can do the same thing we did with David here. Put yourself in their circumstances. Try to feel what they might have been feeling. Make the connections between their struggles and yours. What did they do right? What did they do that dishonored the Lord? Did they grow through their experiences? If so, how? If not, why not? What is the biggest take-away lesson for you?

And why not get yourself a fresh pineapple and dig into that at the same time? When we apply the pineapple principle, rich truths and insights await us, my friend. Never again settle for the canned version of anything.

Part 3

BECOMING MORE THAN A GOOD BIBLE STUDY GIRL

IN MY RELATIONSHIPS

Several years ago I was mistakenly copied on an email I was never meant to see. The harsh tone and biting words of the sender took my breath away, revealing things about this woman's heart that simply broke mine. I couldn't believe what she had said. First, her words weren't true. Second, if she really cared about making things better, she would have come to me instead of weaving a tangled web of lies, destruction, and hurt.

This was a woman who loved the Lord. Yet the same lips that praised Jesus one day cursed me—a fellow sister in Christ—the next. At the root of this entire issue was a misunderstanding that a simple explanation would have cleared up.

I was no saint in this situation either. Had I been operating in the total security of God's love, my hurt would not have been nearly as deep as it was. For weeks, I refused to forgive her until God broke through my stubborn resolve.

Good eventually came from this event. I learned how crucial it is to let God's love, not others' opinions, be the truth out of which I operate, and the other woman learned how destructive envy and angry words can be.

This section on relationships is intended to make us more fully aware of those things that so easily trip us up. Friendships should be one of our greatest assets along this journey with Christ. God created us to do life in community with others, to show and receive love in such a way that captures the world's attention and draws others to Him. Why would we trade God's great and wonderful plan for relationships for anything less?

Becoming more than just good Bible study girls in our relationships means pursuing the richer, deeper possibilities that exist past our own insecurities, unharnessed thoughts, and careless words. I suspect, if you've been hurt in a relationship like most of us have, you are more than ready for a change!

Chapter 7

SHE LIKES ME,
SHE LIKES ME NOT

There was a season of my girlhood in which I was most devoted to a certain book. A book with a plaid cover and big promises. I could often be found curled up in my Kmart comforter devouring this book full of fashion, fun, and cool sayings. It was, of course, *The Official Preppy Handbook*.

After reading it, I'd literally dream in hues of hot pink and kelly green.

It made me want to change my name to Buffy, vacation at Hilton Head, wear madras shorts and Pappagallo flats, tie a grosgrain ribbon in my hair, and use the phrases "like totally" and "gag me with a spoon."

I'd one day marry a man whose first name was Ralph. Ralph Lauren, to be exact. The Ralph who rode around on a horse carrying a polo stick. Yes, him.

We'd have three kids—Biff, Skip, and Muffy—who would live with us until the tender age of three when we'd shoo them off to a college preparatory nursery boarding school somewhere in New York City. But being the caring parents we would surely be, we'd have their nannies drive them out to our English Tudor home in the Hamptons on weekends. There we would school them in the finer arts of Izod shirts, Lilly Pulitzer shift dresses, and the proper rules for playing croquet on the front lawn.

Now, I must insert here, if your name is Buffy, Ralph, Biff, Skip, or Muffy ... or if you wear Polo, Izod, or Pulitzer ... or if you play croquet and have nannies and your kids attend boarding school ... can I just state that I heart you. You are living my childhood dream. Like totally.

Anyhow, back to me, my dreams, and my Kmart comforter.

The Official Preppy Handbook spoke of things in which, how should I say this, our family simply chose not to participate. In other words, we were poor. But there was this one Christmas when I was twelve, right after my parents divorced, that held a most glorious promise.

My dad offered to take me shopping with a whopping budget of $75. It might as well have been $7,500, because in my world a collection of three twenties, a ten, and a fiver was wealth beyond my pink-and-green imagination.

I woke the morning of our shopping trip and put on the one luxury item I had in my wardrobe, my Calvin Klein jumper dress. Never mind the Izod knockoff, white-collared shirt underneath. The metal fastenings that connected the straps of the jumper were the perfect disguise for my no-alligator-emblem shirt.

Me, my jumper, and my excited little preppie wannabe heart jumped into the front seat of my dad's car and headed to the mall. The big one. The one with—suck all the air out of the room right now—a Pappagallo store! Which, thank you very much, had just gotten a new shipment of whale belt buckles and tortoise-shell handled purses with button-on covers.

Oh, how my heart raced. Seeing myself walking the locker-lined halls of Raa Middle School looking as if I'd just stepped straight from the pages of the prepsters guide made a smile spread across my face too wide to properly contain my buck teeth. I was a vision of pure loveliness and joy.

That is, until my dad parked in front of Sears.

I tried to assure my shaky self that he must be getting some tools or tires or towels. We'd get whatever was on his list, then make a beeline to Pappagallo where I'd carefully planned how I would spend every dime of his promised $75 gift.

But as soon as we walked inside, he held up his Sears credit card and told me to have at it. Guessing that Pappagallo might not take kindly to me trying to use a Sears card, I wanted to cry. I did cry. I sat down on that cold linoleum floor and let my emotions have their way.

That tiny plastic card unleashed a flood of much more than tears. Every mean name the popular girls at school had ever called me. Every comment my daddy ever made about not wanting children, especially not a girl. Every family dysfunction we pretended was normal. Every day a frizzy-headed, bucktoothed girl who simply didn't measure up in the eyes of her peers stared back at me from the mirror. It all gushed out in uncontrollable sobs. Right there next to the Craftsman toolboxes.

My dad shoved his Sears credit card back into his wallet and informed me and my emotional outburst that our Christmas shopping trip was officially over.

SHE LIKES ME, SHE LIKES ME NOT

That Christmas shopping day was never about whale belt buckles or tortoise-shell handled purses. Really, my whole love for *The Official Preppy Handbook* was never about fashion, vacation spots, hip names, or cool sayings. I just wanted to be accepted. By someone.

There is a fundamental need inside most girls to be liked.

We want some people of the female variety to totally get us and walk away thinking we are pretty neat. It's like we carry around a miniature scale. On one side we put our coolness and on the other side our total dorkiness.

Put a group of women in a space to mingle for a while and when you release them from that space, I guarantee many will walk away playing that daisy petal game in their head: "She likes me ... she likes me not."

It can take me back to my brace-faced middle school days quicker than Rick Springfield singing "Jessie's Girl." Which, by the way, I totally wanted to be. I didn't have a clue who Jessie was. But to think of Rick pining away, wishing I was his ... sigh.

Those were some good hairbrush-microphone rock concert days. I'd step up onto my bed, hush the vast audience of stuffed animals, and suddenly my bubblegum-pink room was transformed into the downtown civic center. And Rick was totally into me. Braces and all. But eventually I had to step out of my bubblegum-pink room into the pea-green halls of Raa Middle School. Let the mental petal picking games begin.

I talked too much. Dork.

But I did get a laugh from so-and-so. Cool.

So-and-so asked me over to her house. Way cool.

But I spit out that cookie crumb while talking to her. Why did it have to be her? Total dork.

And then the kiss of death ... Popular Patty was having a party and everyone who is anyone was invited. But not me. Dork of epic proportions.

Good thing we've all matured past those middle school days. Long ago we wedged our dork/cool scales between our preppy handbooks and *Grease* albums and tucked them up in the attic somewhere. Right?

External achievement never equals internal acceptance.

Then why do I still find myself bouncing around between feelings of dorkiness and coolness in crowds of people? Because, yes, I still struggle sometimes. May I let you in on a secret? No amount of worldly achievement whisks away insecurities and that fundamental desire to be accepted. I know. I've tried.

Just because you write a few books, speak in front of a few crowds, and achieve what you always thought would make you feel special does not fix that deep-down internal insecurity. External achievement never equals internal acceptance.

And I'm not alone in this. I recently blogged on this topic and received a flood of comments:

> **Kim:** I have experienced everything you wrote about—and still do. I thought it would get better as I got older. I recently turned thirty-five and I still go back and forth between feeling like the dork and the cool kid. UGH!
>
> **April:** My eyes got misty as I read your post today. Man oh man, have I struggled with that. So many times when I have come face-to-face with my insecurities and found myself dwelling in the land of "What if I were skinnier, prettier, more self assured ... would she like me?" I compare my grown-up self to my teenaged self and sigh. Sometimes I don't think I've changed that much at all.
>
> **Jackie:** You have expressed to a "T" exactly what I struggle with anytime I am in a crowd of women. I've never mentioned it to anyone because I was positive I was alone in feeling like a big ol 'dork. I thought if I just did something special, or was SOMEBODY, these feelings would go away.

Can you identify with these feelings of insecurity? I'm not sure we can totally rid ourselves of them. And maybe we're not supposed to. If they press us to draw closer to God, the only secure thing, then healthy doses of insecurity might not be so bad. We'll talk about that more in just a minute. But insecurities that distract and paralyze us at times must be brought into proper perspective. Since these insecurities seem to be rooted in feelings of inadequacy, let's take a look at a healthy way to make peace with all of this.

MAKING PEACE WITH INADEQUACY

If just getting a little older and piling up achievements doesn't help us make peace with our feelings of inadequacy, what will? I've found a two-step process that helps — I must operate *in* God's love and operate *with* God's love.

STEP 1: OPERATE *IN* GOD'S LOVE

Operating *in* God's love means understanding how His love can redefine my natural thought processes. Using God's Word, I can fill my thoughts with His truths to combat the lies tangled around my feelings. Therefore, when I feel insecure, I can combat that feeling with a reassuring and redefining word from God.

If I want to make peace with inadequacy, I must face head-on those things that trigger such feelings, stop looking at others for validation, and learn to truly depend on God. Let's call it like it is and say it out loud:

> I sometimes feel insecure and inadequate. No person or achievement can fix this. Only God can help me, reassure me, and fill up my empty places.

When I feel like that little girl pulling the daisy petals, whispering, "She likes me ... she likes me not," I have to choose to mentally set the flower aside. I'll look up and say, "God, You not only like me, You love me ... and that is enough." You see, I have retrained my brain so God's truths interrupt my negative thought patterns.

It used to be that feelings of insecurity immediately sent my brain back into the same mental ruts I hazarded as a young teen looking in the mirror at my frizzy-headed, imperfect reflection. But I have patched those holes with the permanent fix of God's truths.

Here are some of the verses I have memorized and often quote as a way to help me operate in God's love.

Forget the former things; do not dwell on the past. See, I am doing a new thing! Now it springs up; do you not perceive it? (Isaiah 43:18–19a)

That's the part I have memorized, but the rest of that verse and some of the next two are so good I'm working on them too:

I am making a way in the desert and streams in the wasteland . . . to give drink to my people, my chosen, the people I formed for myself that they may proclaim my praise. (43:19b, 20b–21)

These verses remind me that a new way of processing my feelings of inadequacy is possible. Just because such feelings have negatively affected me and held me back in the past doesn't mean that's the way it will always be.

Though the mountains be shaken and the hills be removed, yet my unfailing love for you will not be shaken. (Isaiah 54:10)

My feelings of inadequacy are often rooted in a fear of failing. Isaiah 54:10 reminds me that no amount of failure or falling short will change God's love for me. This comforting reality helps me to not shy away from hard things but to press into God's strength and operate with more courage.

And so we know and rely on the love God has for us. (1 John 4:16)

This verse reminds me that while people can prove unreliable, God never is. It is possible to know Him in deeper ways than human relationships and learn to rely on His love to stabilize the places we fall short.

Like the rest of the Bible, all these verses are God's truth. Recite them. Repeat them. Recall them as often as necessary. And remember the key words in these verses: God is doing a new thing in us. We are chosen people; chosen, as in handpicked by God. God's love is unfailing despite what we do or don't do. His love is completely reliable.

And these are but a tiny sampling of the many verses that refer to God's thoughts about us and His great love for us. Sometimes I have to quote these Scriptures ten, twenty, a hundred times ... but I keep saying them until the truth seeps in and I can leave the petal-pulling behind.

The Bible also says in 1 John 4:19, "We love because he first loved us." If we rearrange the two thoughts in this verse, watch what happens: "Because he first loved us ... we love." Which leads us to the second step that helps me overcome feelings of inadequacy: operating *with* God's love.

STEP 2: OPERATE *WITH* GOD'S LOVE

Operating *with* God's love allows me to rest in a security beyond myself. It's okay that I'm insecure if it prompts me to rely on God more fully. When I try to live life only relying on myself, any insecurity seems like a disadvantage. But when I operate with God's love, I ask Him to show me how to use my insecurities to my advantage rather than my disadvantage.

Again, let's say this out loud together:

Insecurities should not prompt me to *get* things from others that I should be getting from God. Rather they should prompt me to *give* to others so I can point them to God.

My insecurities can actually help me if I allow God to use them to make me more sensitive and discerning toward the insecurities of others. If I can sense when someone needs an encouraging word, a hug (which is big because I'm not a huggy person), a comment on their blog, or a quick email, then that is a positive way to use my insecurities to my advantage — or, better yet, to God's advantage.

In his book *The Search for Significance*, Robert McGee writes:

> The fear of rejection is rampant, and loneliness is one of the most dangerous and widespread problems in America today.... Loneliness is not relegated only to unbelievers. Ninety-two percent of the Christians attending a recent Bible conference admitted in a survey that feelings of loneliness were a major problem in their lives. All shared a basic symptom: a sense of despair at feeling unloved and a fear of being unwanted or unaccepted. This is a tragic commentary on the people about whom Christ said: *By this all men will know that you are my disciples, if you love one another* (John 13:35).[4]

That quote challenges me and makes me realize how many of us are dealing with the exact same negative feelings. We aren't alone!

Can you imagine what might happen if we let God show us how to use our insecurities and feelings of inadequacy as His prompts to love others more? I mean, really think about the simplicity of simply loving others and yet the absolute profound impact that it could make.

And it *is* possible.

One of Satan's greatest tools to hold us back from telling the world about Christ is to get us to put our sense of security in the wrong place. Jesus never meant for evangelism to be complicated and hard. He simply instructed us to love Him and love others (Matthew 22:37 – 39). I like the way 1 John 4:11 – 12 puts it: "Dear friends, since God so loved us, we also ought to love one another. No one has ever seen God; but if we love one another, God lives in us and his love is made complete in us."

When we love others, we are living the truth of God out loud. Since every person needs love, it may open the door for us to share that God is the source for our love. Can you think of someone who could use a touch of love right now? When you consider the opportunities all around you, it will rock your world more than if Pappagallo suddenly let shoppers use a Sears credit card at their store.

*When we love others, we are living
the truth of God out loud.*

How do my insecurities, inadequacies and feelings of dorkiness prompt me to love? What does this look like on a practical, everyday level?

Sometimes I'll wake up during the night and think of someone I know who is in pain, which prompts me to pray for them. It's a choice.

In a roomful of people, I can pick up on a person who feels overlooked by others and my heart is more sensitive to notice them. It's a choice.

Or if some stranger is really rude to me, instead of getting miffed, I try to see their humanness apart from their action. If I pause for just a moment, I can remember that under the tough exterior there's a good chance a war of insecurities is raging within their heart. It's a choice.

I'm also slower to judge others. Instead of criticizing, I try to intentionally look for things that are good about them and park my mind there. It's a choice.

If I was totally secure in myself all the time, I don't think it would increase my qualifications for ministry. As a matter of fact, I think it would do exactly the opposite. So, in essence, my feeling like a dork sometimes is actually a gift. A gift that should lead me to operate *in* God's love and *with* God's love.

Oh, and just so you know, I am in another season of my girlhood in which I am most devoted to a certain book. A book with a soft leather cover and big promises. I can often be found curled up in my Wal-Mart comforter devouring this book full of truth, comfort, and life change. It is, of course, *The Official Holy Bible.*

Chapter 8

BUT I WANT WHAT SHE HAS

I grew up poor. The kind of poor where you had to get creative with everything.

While other kids played in the backyard on their shiny metal swing sets from Kmart, we had to play in a ditch behind our low-rent apartment complex.

While other kids were decorating their pink plastic Barbie houses, I was decorating a shoebox that would have to do. I remember finding a great treasure one day in a patch of lush, mossy-green ground cover. I could cut out squares of it, lay it in my box and, for a day or two, pretend my Barbie house had the most awesome green shag carpet around. Then it eventually turned brown and back out to the woods I'd go in search of new carpet.

And there was no such thing as a weeklong beach vacation. We had beach *days*. Since we lived in Florida, the beach was never more than a couple hours' drive. We'd pile into the un-air-conditioned red Pinto with the black plastic leatherette seats and head to the shore. Equipped with nothing but hand-sewn bathing suits and a big bag of Doritos for each kid, we'd spend all day jumping the waves and digging in the sand.

The drives home are among my most favorite memories. There's nothing quite like the way sandy, salty, sunburned skin sticks to black plastic leatherette seats—hot, un-air-conditioned, black plastic leatherette seats.

Strangely, I don't remember feeling deprived one bit. What we lacked in resources and convenience we more than made up for with our imaginations.

I thought I was the luckiest girl alive.

Who wanted a metal swing set when you could have a ditch? Some days it was the Grand Canyon that we dared each other to leap across. Other days it was a palace in which we set up house and served high tea. On rainy days it was a swimming pool with a rich supply of mud bombs.

Who'd want a store-bought Barbie house with confining plastic rooms when you could have the flexibility of the shoebox variety? One day Barbie was in a one-box ranch; the next day she married J. R. Ewing and had a four-box mansion. Bummer on the third day when someone shot J. R. and she had to settle in a two-box split-level.

And who would ever want to spend a whole week at the beach? My skin was so burned after one day I couldn't fathom any more than that. Those poor people who had to go sleep in motels. We got to load up in the Pinto, blast our Commodores eight-track cassette music, and let our hair whip every which way as we sped home.

Then after a bath and hearty dinner of boxed macaroni and cheese, I'd slip under my Holly Hobby sheets and dream up what my ditch could become tomorrow.

Eventually, we moved from our apartment into a small yellow ranch with brown trim. It wasn't much, but it was ours. This meant I could paint my bedroom. Glory of all glories, my mom agreed to let me pick the color: bubblegum pink.

I thought I'd died and gone to heaven.

That is, until the day I realized we were poor.

AN ERODING DISCONTENTMENT

I was at school one day putting some books back on the shelf by the big window in our classroom. The classroom overlooked the front of the school and, because the school was not air-conditioned, the window was open. Longing to be outside playing instead of inside reading, I lingered there and took my time finishing the job.

Suddenly my daydream was interrupted by a strange and unusual sight. A long black car pulled into the parking lot and stopped at the end of the front walkway. Out hopped a beautiful, black-haired girl who looked to be about my age. Two men wearing sunglasses accompanied her. They were busy fidgeting with walkie-talkies and scanning a stack of papers when they suddenly realized the girl had gotten quite ahead and was about to enter the building without them.

I watched in amazement as they ran to catch up and made a fuss over opening the door for her. Soon they were out of my line of sight, but, oh, how I wanted to know more. I couldn't wait until recess. I had some investigating to do.

It turned out that the new governor of our state had a girl of elementary school age—a beautiful, black-haired girl, to be exact. And she'd been assigned to attend our school. Though they tried to make her seem like everybody else, we all knew she was special.

At first I avoided her. I couldn't imagine we'd have much in common. Her long-black-car world, complete with shiny windows and bodyguards, seemed a far cry from my latchkey-kid world, complete with a scratched-up pink Huffy bike.

But one day over lunch we met. I don't remember what she ate, but I clearly remember what I had. Since I didn't like peanut butter but desperately wanted to bring sandwiches on white bread that looked like the cool kids' PB&Js, my mom made me grape-jelly-and-sliced-cheese sandwiches. No one ever suspected my little ruse. But the beautiful, black-haired girl called my bluff right away and told me she thought it was cool.

Before too long we were friends. Friends who wanted to get together outside of school. Imagine the look on my mom's face when I told her I'd been invited to the governor's mansion to play. We pulled up to the gated fence surrounding a huge brick house, got buzzed through by security, parked our little red Pinto out front, and were escorted through the stately white front doors.

Inside that mansion, I was blown away by the things that gleamed and were called by names that escaped my vocabulary. It wasn't the fancy artwork, or the marbled floors, or the statues created by famous artists that tugged at my contentment. It was my friend's ability to get what she wanted when she wanted it that lured my heart away from feeling like the lucky little girl I'd always been.

Suddenly I noticed things about my surroundings that had never bothered me before. Her sheets were smooth; mine were nubby. Her clothes were fashionable and expensive; mine were cheap. Her toys were kept in a huge closet full of shelves and organizers; mine were strewn randomly around my room. She had a whole closet that served as her baby dolls' nursery; my baby dolls had make-shift beds.

Though she never pointed out our differences and was one of my most gracious friends, my comparisons became an eroding discontentment. I don't remember the first time I heard the word "poor," but I do remember the shift that happened in my heart when I started to feel the weight of what that meant in my life.

I assumed my friend lacked for nothing. My life was peppered with evidences of lack. I did what too many people do when they hold themselves up against another person and walk away feeling deprived: I started resenting my life. I stopped looking for the good in my situation or appreciating what I did have.

AM I EQUIPPED TO HANDLE IT?

See if you can you relate to any of these scenarios:

My house looks great until a friend redecorates. Her clever color combination and crafty restoration abilities have created rooms that look straight from a magazine. Suddenly my home feels outdated and plain.

My kids seem great until I'm around someone else's kids who excel in areas my kids don't. I see her kids quietly reading books that are well advanced for their age and loving every minute of it. My kids would rather have their right arms cut off than read books that are barely grade level, all the while asking me when they can go do something else more exciting. Suddenly I feel like a sub-par mom and berate myself for not making reading more of a priority when they were younger.

Whenever I get an overly idyllic view of someone else's circumstances, I often remind myself out loud, "I am not equipped to handle what they have—both good and bad."

My marriage is wonderful until I see a movie starring a Mr. Right character who is the perfect blend of romance, conversation, fashion, and compassion. I compare him to my outdoorsy, T-shirt wearing man who doesn't believe pain exists in the absence of blood ... and I sigh.

In each scenario, every blessing I thought I enjoyed suddenly pales in comparison. I'm blinded to what I do have in the face of what I lack, my heart drawn to a place of both assumption and ungratefulness. I *assume* that everything is great for those who possess what I don't have, and that assumption causes me to become *less thankful* for what I do have.

And here's the kicker ... things for the person I'm comparing myself to are almost never what they seem. If there's one thing that living forty years has taught me, it's that everybody has not-so-great aspects of their lives. That's why whenever I get an overly idyllic view of someone else's circumstances, I often remind myself out loud, "I am not equipped to handle what they have—both good and bad."

The Good and the Bad

When I want the good thing someone has, I must realize that I'm also asking for the bad that comes along with it. It's always a package deal. And usually if I just give a situation enough time to unfold, I thank God I didn't get someone else's package.

One of the first times I came to understand this truth was in middle school when I met a beautiful girl at the children's theater in my town. We were both budding child actors cast in a Christmas play. During rehearsals I remember feeling envious that her long dancer's legs could move in ways my stubby limbs never would. Her legs were muscular and lean and graceful; mine couldn't be described with any of those adjectives.

One day she felt an unusual pain in her left leg. A doctor's appointment turned into a battery of tests that turned into a hospital stay that turned into a diagnosis. Cancer. A surgery to remove a tumor turned into an amputation turned into a complete life change. Her world became filled with words no child should ever have to know: chemotherapy, prosthetics, hair loss, and walking canes.

As a young girl I was stunned by the whole thing. Especially because I clearly remember night after night watching her glide across the stage and asking God for legs exactly like hers.

Not equipped to handle what they have—both good and bad.

In my early married years I met an older woman who was one of the calmest souls I'd ever encountered. It seriously appeared as though she and her husband had never once had an argument or even a slight disagreement.

I wanted her patience, her grace, her gentleness. I always felt like I had firecrackers in my blood when my husband and I disagreed; I became very vocal and wanted to talk it out at grand decibel levels. Our communication felt like a rip-roaring boxing match compared to the other couple's well choreographed waltz.

One day I confessed to her that I wished my marriage were just like hers. That's when she reached across the table and described the high price she and her husband had paid for the communication they now shared. Early in their marriage, her husband had an affair which nearly ruined their relationship and almost destroyed her as a person. It took years of counseling to rebuild the devastating effects of his betrayal.

Not equipped to handle what they have—both good and bad.

Several years ago I was asked to speak at a conference with several other women whom I considered to be much bigger names than me. I sat in the green room and almost peed in my pants each time one of them introduced themselves. I was hyperconscious of every word I said and every move I made. Talk about reverting back to those middle school feelings at warp speed. Sakes alive!

One speaker glided in with an entourage. Boy, did she ever have it all together. While I had been staining my outfit with sweat while setting up my own book table, she'd been getting her hair and makeup done. An assistant had set up her book table.

My hair was a mess, my makeup had melted away, and I was afraid my deodorant would soon fail me. Oh, if only I had her success, I wouldn't have to walk out on stage looking and feeling like such a complete wreck.

I later found out she'd just received news that the company that sponsored the arena events she'd been doing for over ten years had cancelled her contract.

Not equipped to handle what they have—both good and bad.

I don't want to paint the picture that every good circumstance someone else has automatically ends in tragedy. That's not the case. Sometimes the good things that happen to people are simply fantastic. But they are fantastic for them, not me.

Not equipped to handle what they have—both good and bad.

REDIRECTED THOUGHTS

When I find myself making comparisons and wanting what someone else has, I must consciously choose to redirect my thinking. Too many of us live with an uncontrolled thought life. It is possible to learn to identify destructive thoughts and make wiser choices. Instead of letting these thoughts rumble freely about in my mind, I make the choice to harness them and direct them toward truth.

Too many of us live with
an uncontrolled thought life.

Think of something you want that someone else has. Have you been lured into thinking, "If only I had _____ like that person, my life would be great!"

Now, practice redirecting those thoughts by saying instead:

I am not equipped for her good.
I am not equipped for her bad.
I am not equipped to carry the weight of her victories.
I am not equipped to shoulder her burdens.
I am not equipped to be her in any way.
I am, however, perfectly equipped to be me.
Therefore, thank You, God, for only entrusting me with what
    I have and who I am.

When I compare myself to others and focus on wanting what they have, it quite simply wears me out trying to figure out how to have more, be more, and do more. That's why Jesus instructs worn-out people, "Come to me, all you who are weary and burdened, and I will give you rest. Take my yoke upon you and learn from me, for I am gentle and humble in heart, and you will find rest for your souls. For my yoke is easy and my burden is light" (Matthew 11:28–30).

Note a couple key words in these verses. A "yoke" is a wooden frame used to harness two draft animals to whatever they have to pull. The Greek word for "easy" can also mean "well-fitted." Combine this information together and it appears that Jesus is saying He has equipped each of us with well-fitted assignments in life. As long as we do and aspire to only what He calls us, our burden will not only be manageable, it will be light.

It's also interesting to note that when an animal is in training, a farmer will often put it in a head yoke rather than a neck yoke to keep the animal from looking around and getting anxious. I think my head yoke has been the thought-redirecting statement, "I'm not equipped to handle what they have — both good and bad." It sure has stopped me from looking around and getting anxious!

SHE WANTS WHAT I HAVE

I recently received a letter that started by saying, "Lysa, I've been insanely jealous of you since meeting you at my women's retreat over three years ago. I've wanted your ministry to be my ministry, your books to be my books, your speaking engagements to be my speaking engagements, and your faith to be my faith. Each time this ugly jealousy oozed up in my heart, I made excuses for its existence and tried to push it out of sight. But it hasn't gone away."

My heart broke.

I understand that parts of my life may seem glamorous. But on the underside of the speaking engagements and published books is the reality of a lot of hard work, late nights, and sacrifices. Tears at 3:00 a.m. after staying up to meet a deadline. Missing my friend's birthday lunch because of a previously scheduled radio recording. A delayed flight that forced me to spend the night at Chicago O'Hare. Judgments from those who think I can't be a good mother because I travel out of town.

Things that are a burden, but a burden for which I have been equipped, therefore making it manageable. *But oh, sweet sister, do not pine away wishing my assignment was yours.*

She went on to tell me that the Lord challenged her to read one of my books with a Bible study. She had avoided my books in the past. But in this act of obedience, God met her through this study. Her letter continued, "But the greatest gift so far has been the realization the Lord gave me this morning: I am not jealous of you personally, Lysa, or all that God has accomplished through you. I have been jealous of your faith. I've had this delusional notion that your faith was handed to you by God, and that somehow I got shortchanged. But God debunked that wrong thinking today. He showed me clearly that He's got plans for my faith to be as deep, real, strong, and fervent as yours.... It's all a process, as you've written. God couldn't give me your ministry, your books, your speaking opportunities, because it wasn't meant for me."

Amazing. Relieving. Confirming.

God had been working behind the scenes in her life. He was whispering through her comparisons, jealousies, and feelings of being somehow shortchanged by Him with the same truth with which He'd comforted me many times.

Not equipped to handle what they have—both good and bad.

It's true of the young girl with a pink Huffy bike as well as a forty-year-old woman with a messy, sweaty speaking outfit. It's true for my letter-writing friend. And it's true for you too if you ever catch yourself saying, "But I want what she has."

Chapter 9

CROSS MY HEART AND CLOSE MY MOUTH

Bright purple lips, sticky droplets on our shoes, and two wooden sticks were all telltale signs of three glorious truths. It was summer. My mom had remembered to fill and freeze our homemade ice tray popsicles. And my most special friend in the world had come over.

Boy, did I ever need to have a little heart-to-heart talk with Sally.

While the sun baked down on us, my heart started racing. How do you share a secret? Would she keep it to herself? It took me the entire popsicle to get up the courage. When my tongue had nothing but a stick left to lick, I knew it was time to open up my insides and let a little bit spill out.

Sally and I made a promise with two entwined pinky fingers. I knew my heart was safe with her. We were two girls taking those last few steps of childhood together. Right there in the midst of a normal summer day, we started to grow up. It wasn't long until we laid down our popsicle sticks and jumped into a new season of life.

The secret I shared in a hushed conversation was about a boy at school with brown hair and brown eyes whose mom drove a brown car through the carpool line. I've never liked the color brown so much in my whole life. He wore Izod shirts with the collar flipped up in back. Both Sally and I had suspicions his curls weren't natural. Just imagining him with a towel around his neck while his mom put permanent rods in his hair made us laugh so hard our sides ached.

Everything about Sally was cool, even the way she got her name. She was a true blend of her parents. Her father's name was Sal and her mom's name was Lee. They were the most loving couple I'd ever seen.

It was Sally who first introduced me to Miracle Whip, Cabbage Patch dolls, and how to hot roll your hair even when it's cut in a mullet. Bless her. And now she gave me the total scoop on how to have a crush on a boy. She was, after all, quite the expert. Not that she'd had a crush. She had not. But she did have an older sister who not only had a crush but had actually had a boy kiss her on the cheek!

Instead of thinking boys were gross and stinky and should be avoided at all costs, I had just admitted that all of life would be hearts and roses if only that boy with the brown curly hair would look my way. Oh, what a scandalous little secret that was!

Sally could have so easily judged me with this admission. Just months before we'd both declared that we'd never like boys ... EVER! She could have gained favor with some of the more popular girls by gossiping my news. It might have gained her instant access to the in-crowd. And she certainly could have chastised me for wanting to go against our normal grain and talk on and on about all things boy related.

But Sally never did any of that. She loved me. And she never used my words against me. She just stuck out her pinkie and grabbed hold of mine. Once again we intertwined our little fingers as a sign and a promise to never betray one another's trust.

Sally and I remained close friends all the way through high school. Though we rarely see each other now, Sally will never leave me. She never betrayed that pinky promise shared over a popsicle ... or any of the hundreds of other secrets we shared. She protected those vulnerable places of my heart. My childhood secrets are still locked tightly away in her heart and hers in mine.

A friend who guards her words is a gift. I am forever grateful I had this precious childhood friend. Later in life, when I was betrayed by friends' words, knowing what true friendship could be became an anchor of hope for my soul.

A friend who guards her words is a gift.

A WAY WITH WORDS

When Sally and I made pinky promises to one another, we often sealed the deal with the phrase, "Cross my heart." Those three little words were the container for a big promise. Unfortunately, this same statement can represent a world of hurt if a friend literally crosses your heart and leaves you feeling betrayed.

Words spoken by friends are especially powerful. They can lift us up and spur us on to achieve things that wouldn't have been possible without the encouragement of a friend. But hurtful words can also be the very thing that renders a woman powerless and shuts her down.

The letters and emails I've gotten from women telling me of their devastating experiences with hurtful words spoken by people they thought were friends grieve my heart. And even more so, women hurting other women grieves God's heart.

I'm sure I don't need to share the gory details of how careless words have broken apart friendships. If you're like me, you've probably been hurt deeply more times than you care to recall. And if we are brutally honest, we also can probably think of times when we ourselves have been a lousy friend and caused hurt in another's life.

Of all the things we'll talk about when it comes to being more than a good Bible study girl, this might just be one of the most challenging. But it's also the exact lesson through which Jesus wants to do a beautiful work in our hearts. Just a brief glance through the Gospels reveals why loving others is so high on Jesus' priority list for us. For example, "A new command I give you: Love one another. As I have loved you, so you must love one another. By this all men will know that you are my disciples, if you love one another" (John 13:34–35). It is simply impossible to love another person the way Christ wants us to love while speaking hurtful words to or about them. And loving others isn't a gentle suggestion by Jesus—it's a command. Since our words are such a crucial indication of whether or not we love someone, we would do well to carefully watch what we say.

The woman who is more than a good Bible study girl is so secure in her relationship with Jesus that the graceful way she interacts with others makes following Him look appealing. People can trust her Jesus because she has proven herself to be trustworthy. Her witness for Christ is powerful and effective because her words are saturated with His authentic love. Now that is a woman other women want to be around!

For others to meet the reality of Jesus in our lives, we must be women of carefully chosen words. There is just no way around this and no justification for not doing it. What comes out of our mouths is a telltale sign of who we are, who we serve, and what we truly believe. It requires that we refuse to gossip, choose not to judge, and become secure in our unique calling.

What comes out of our mouths is a telltale sign of who we are, who we serve, and what we truly believe.

REFUSE TO GOSSIP

One day I got a phone message from a neighbor named Holly. She said that she knew I liked to run and suggested I give her a call if I ever wanted a running partner. What I didn't know until much later is that God had been prompting her to call me and wouldn't let up until she did.

Holly and I did start running together and what began as a simple act of obedience on her part developed into a deep friendship. This was a huge answer to prayer, because I had been praying for a friend exactly like Holly. Not only is Holly one of my closest friends, but she is also now my executive assistant. In other words, she keeps me straight on many levels, and I love every minute of it.

One day Holly gave me a unique gift that made my heart feel forever safe with her. Though it wasn't costly to her, it became priceless to me. She committed to me that she would never say anything dishonoring about me. It was more than just a commitment to me; it was a covenant promise she'd made with God. I can't even express what peace this brought to my heart.

It's not that I feared my other friends were gossiping about me. I did not. And I can't say that my other friends wouldn't make this same promise. They probably would. But Holly verbalized this commitment boldly—in a way that has defined our friendship and built a beautiful trust rare between women.

Deep, unreserved trust is hard for me. When my dad left my family, something inside of me died. I became raw, sensitive, and fearful of being betrayed again. Later, when my sister died and my mom's grief swept over her like a suffocating blanket, I couldn't shake the feeling I wasn't good enough to make my mom happy again. I felt betrayed all over again by the only parent who'd ever really cared about me. It was an unfair assumption to make about my mom, but my dad's betrayal had tainted my perspective. The deepest parts of me resisted close relationships. Way too risky.

Finding out that someone had gossiped about me or judged me ushered me right back to that little girl standing in the front window of my house, watching my dad drive away. Someone who was supposed to protect me had just reopened the wound.

Since we know the tsunami-type destruction gossip can cause, why is carelessly tossing out hurtful words about others so alluring? Gossip is easy to slip into and hard to walk away from. If we just assume we won't be tempted to gossip, we are fooling ourselves and potentially setting ourselves up for trouble. Verbalizing to a friend that she can trust we will never betray her puts action to three crucial rules the Bible teaches us about our words.

Guard your tongue to keep out of trouble. A wise man named Solomon once said, "He who guards his mouth and his tongue keeps himself from calamity" (Proverbs 21:23). I've found it's not good to be in situations in which idle chatter abounds.

Before I get together with friends, I do two things: I consciously decide not to utter a negative comment or "piece" of gossip I might have heard, and I prepare in advance some positive discussion items. Instead of hoping conversation with friends goes in a healthy direction, why not help steer the conversation?

Limit your words to be wise. That wise guy Solomon also said, "When words are many, sin is not absent, but he who holds his tongue is wise" (Proverbs 10:19). Without a doubt, I love to talk; however, I try to limit the number of words I say. This can be hard when I want to jump in and add my two cents to every conversation. But I've found the fewer the words I speak, the more intentional I can be with the words I do say.

We've developed a practice in our family of asking ourselves three questions before speaking: "Are my words kind? Are they true? Are they necessary?" As I've taught my kids this principle, it's reminded me to continue to implement it in my own life. Can you think of a situation where this could have saved you from trouble? I know I can.

Use your words to validate your relationship with the Lord, not negate it. The Bible teaches there is a clear connection between how we use our words and the validity of our beliefs. According to James 1:26, "If anyone considers himself religious and yet does not keep a tight rein on his tongue, he deceives himself and his religion is worthless."

I'm not a big fan of thinking of my relationship with the Lord as "religious," but this verse powerfully warns me against uncontrolled, thoughtless conversation. It breaks my heart to think my careless words might give others the impression that my relationship with Jesus is worthless.

Do you remember the question I asked in the introduction of this book, "Does Jesus work?" James 1:26 warns us how dangerous it is not to keep a keen watch on our words. If we don't, we appear like hypocrites whose Jesus does not work. Ouch.

I could go on and on about why we shouldn't gossip and give more tips on avoiding it, but the bottom line is, don't do it. Plain and simple. It's not who we are. Not only should I *choose* not to gossip, but I need to choose to believe that *in Christ* I am not a gossiper.

Imagine the number of relationship issues that would simply vanish if we were all more committed to loving words. Why not commit today to make this kind of love a reality with those you care about?

Not only was I encouraged by Holly's commitment to never say anything dishonoring about me, I was challenged by it as well.

Would you like to join me in accepting this challenge by making the same promise? It not only makes friendships richer but, more importantly, it makes our relationship with the Lord more authentic and believable. We honor God when we honor each other. Refusing to gossip is a rare and beautiful gift. One that will make people notice a tangible difference in us because we know the Lord.

Choose Not to Judge

Refusing to gossip is vitally important, but it's not the only thing God requires of us. We can say nothing but still harbor a judgmental spirit, and being judgmental is often what fuels gossip in the first place. A judgment is our assumption that what another person is doing is wrong. And finding someone else to agree with us is what makes gossip so intriguing. We feel superior when we judge other people. Gossiping about them with others somehow makes us feel justified.

My friend Melanie Chitwood wrote a Proverbs 31 Ministries devotion that acknowledges her own struggle in this area and how she is overcoming it:

I've been thinking lately about how easy it is to judge others or to think I have the answers for others. For example, when I see a mother frustrated by her unruly kids, I might think, "She just needs to put those kids in a long time-out." Another time I observe a couple having trouble in their marriage and I question their commitment to God's ways.

In a nutshell, I can be self-righteous, just like the Pharisees. God has been making me aware lately of some of the unspoken yardsticks by which I measure others, such as: A good mom doesn't let her kids watch too much TV and doesn't scream at her kids. Or, a godly woman has a quiet time every day and doesn't fight with her husband.

But then there's Jesus who turns these notions upside down when He says, "The greatest of these is love." What if instead of self-righteousness, we rained down love? It would sound like this: "Being a mom can be exhausting. Do you want to come over and hang out for a while?" or "I've had struggles in my marriage too. Do you want to talk about it?"

God is challenging me to examine my spoken and unspoken judgments of others. He wants us to come alongside others and help carry their burdens, rather than add to them with our criticism. Where the Pharisees heap coals of judgment, Jesus calls us to be vessels of His love and encouragement.[5]

Oh, how I wish someone would have taken this approach with me when I had small children! I sweated over people staring and rolling their eyes when my toddlers acted like toddlers in public. Never once did someone offer to help me. If they had, it surely would have blessed me. Instead of lamenting over what didn't happen, I will use this as a reminder to be more compassionate and helpful to others. There are so many ways I can refuse to be judgmental and rain down love instead!

The Pharisees in Jesus' day prided themselves on their strict adherence to God's laws and harshly judged anyone not like them. They totally disregarded Jesus' teachings on loving others. Interestingly enough, the word "Pharisee" is from the Hebrew word *prushim*, meaning "separated." And they were indeed separated—separated from truth, others, and even God Himself.

When we judge others, we sin. There's just no glossy way to say it. We also separate ourselves from truth, others, and, most tragically, even God Himself. Jesus said, "Do not judge, or you too will be judged. For in the same way you judge others, you will be judged, and with the measure you use, it will be measured to you. Why do you look at the speck of sawdust in your brother's eye and pay no attention to the plank in your own eye?" (Matthew 7:1–3). We may think that judging others is okay as long as we keep it to ourselves, but that's not true. Judging others, according to this verse, not only causes a separation from God's best for us, but it also opens the door for judgments to be cast against us. It's like sending out invitations!

Often we slip into judging others under the guise of being honest enough to say the hard things to a friend. The Bible makes it clear that honesty is important—but so is prayerful consideration of how and when to say things. Saying something hard to someone is not an off-the-cuff assignment. We have to be willing to do life with this person for a while. We have to get a little dirty on their behalf, get to know what their life is really like, and earn the right to have these types of conversations with them.

This is one of my favorite aspects of my friendship with Renee. We work together. We play together. We believe the best about each other, and we are committed to never dishonor one another. We've made so many positive deposits in each other's lives that we have room for constructive criticism without the threat of bankrupting our relationship.

Recently I went through a situation where I needed to make a tough decision, but kept putting it off. As I talked over the matter with Renee, she both encouraged and challenged me. To be honest, I didn't want to hear some of what she said. She disagreed with some of my viewpoints. But, in the end, I knew I could trust her advice, so I made the choice to let her input expand my perspective rather than hurt my feelings. Renee picked the right time to have this conversation and chose words that dealt with the situation rather than judging me. I wound up being better for having a friend who had earned the right to say something hard to me.

But you had better believe that even in this type of friendship, we weigh our constructive criticisms very carefully. We must remember what Jesus said in Matthew 7:1–3: before we can judge someone else we need to first ask God to reveal our own sin. This isn't just for the purpose of cleansing our own impurities, though that is vitally important. It also puts us in a humble position before we approach others. When we are truly humble, we are less likely to be judgmental.

We must always remember the purpose for constructive criticism is not so we can judge others but to help them grow closer to God. Not to make their lives and their opinions more like ours, but more like His.

After we refuse to gossip and choose not to judge, there is still one more task before us: we must learn to be secure in our unique calling.

Be Secure in Your Unique Calling

One day I ran into a friend at the grocery store. After a few minutes of simple chitchat, I commented about needing to help my child finish a project that night because I'd be away speaking at a conference for the weekend. Suddenly her tone changed as she blurted out, "I don't know how you can possibly be okay with leaving your kids like that." I don't remember any other details of our conversation after that, only that the weight of her words just about choked the life out of me. It wasn't the first time someone had questioned me in this way. But I was caught so off guard, I became convinced the whole world was against me. My heart and spirit were crushed.

I came home and grabbed my Bible. *Jesus,* I prayed, *I am so tired of being questioned about this. Every time it makes me discouraged. But this time I just simply want to quit! Please show me something in Your Word that either smacks me in the face with the reality that I need to quit doing ministry or show me something that confirms I should keep on.*

I opened my Bible and found myself reading about the rich young ruler in Luke 18. Honestly, I was a little bummed because I didn't see how my answer would come from this story I'd read many times before. Just as I was about to turn to another chapter I got to verses 29 and 30 at the end of the story, "I tell you the truth," Jesus said to them, "no one who has left home or wife or brothers or parents or children for the sake of the kingdom of God will fail to receive many times as much in this age and, in the age to come, eternal life."

I was stunned. I wanted to write this Scripture on a big old piece of poster board, tuck it in my purse, and whip it out the next time I saw grocery-store-judgment woman. I pictured myself waving it high above my head while saying, "I love my Jesus and I love my family, and it's good, sister. It's all good."

Okay, so maybe I didn't actually picture myself calling her "sister." I may or may not have been tempted to call her "meanie head." But since I am clearly writing a chapter on watching our words, I am making the choice to call her "sister." See, I'm learning.

In the following weeks I continued to seek God's confirmation. Then I came across a blog written by a woman whose calling is very different than mine; however, her conviction is the same. Elizabeth is a dear woman whose calling is to homeschool her ten kids, but she too is bothered by how women hurt women.

We eat our own. We make up litmus tests and then level judgments. Does she dress the way a Christian woman should? Does she wear her hair the way a Christian woman should?

Does she go to the "right" parish or church? Does she manage her finances the "right" way? Spend her time the "right" way? Does she have enough children and are they spaced the "right" way? If the answers don't fit what we've decided constitute holiness, we chew the woman up and spit her out in disgust.

And we become women of opinion, not conviction, to use a phrase coined by Colleen Mitchell. We become women who are so preoccupied by judging and condemning that we tear down our *own* homes with our own hands. The spirit of condemnation pervades the very being of the woman and erodes at the gentleness, peacefulness, and goodness her family deserves. She becomes a bitter woman and her life bears bitter fruit.[6]

Maybe you've struggled with being that bitter woman who struggles holding back her gossip and judgments of others. God calls women to make a difference in this world. Whatever corner of the world He's called us to, we must find joy there and resist the urge to make our way of doing life the only way. When we let our mind go to places it shouldn't, it is doubly hard to hold back the judgment and the gossip.

Maybe you've been hurt by a bitter woman of opinion. Whether you work outside the home, work from the home, or make running your home your occupation; whether your kids are public schooled, private schooled, or homeschooled; whether you remain single, get married, or join the circus and live on the road—do it to the glory of God! As long as you are in the place God has called you and He's using you, then rest secure in that and let others' criticisms roll off your back. Believe me, I know how hard it is to do this. But I also know how freeing it can be.

Refusing to gossip, choosing not to judge, and remaining secure in our own calling will pave the way to the types of friendships we all desire. While I am very blessed with the friends I have, I will tell you I've been through some very tough seasons of loneliness, betrayal, hurt, and grief. If you struggle with being surrounded by friends like we've discussed in this chapter, please spend some time praying that God would bless this area of your life. In the meantime, be the kind of friend you desperately want. God will eventually honor your desire and bless you with friends who refuse to gossip, choose not to judge, and who are secure enough in their own calling not to hold you back in yours.

Be the kind of friend you desperately want.
God will eventually honor your desire.

SEEING GOD'S BIGGER PLAN FOR FRIENDSHIPS

God has a beautiful plan for people to work together; learning to use our words well is a big part of that. We would be wise to heed the apostle Paul's words, "Do not let any unwholesome talk come out of your mouths, but only what is helpful for building others up according to their needs, that it may benefit those who listen" (Ephesians 4:29). We are uniquely designed to be drawn to certain people in friendship. The reasons extend beyond just doing life together. We are called to build each other up so we can help one another serve God most effectively.

We can choose to promote cooperation that builds God's kingdom rather than engage in criticism that tears it apart. If telling the world about Jesus is our real goal, then we must be eager to cooperate with the unique ways God leads people to make this happen. If, however, our goal is to prove that our way of living the Christian life is the only way, then we suddenly become women with critical eyes and sharp tongues who compare everyone else to our misguided standards.

"A landmark UCLA study suggests friendships between women are special. They shape who we are and who we are yet to be. They

soothe our tumultuous inner world, fill the emotional gaps in our marriage, and help us remember who we really are."[7] What a gift!

Why would we ever want to trade in the beauty of all that friendship has to offer for just a few careless words? Maybe we'd all do well
to grab a popsicle, show up on the front steps of our friend's house, and
spend a few minutes intertwining our pinky fingers and promising to
never gossip, judge, or become a distraction from God's calling. Cross
our heart and close our mouths.

Part 4

IN MY STRUGGLES

I could have gone in so many different directions when writing this section, for I am a woman with both high hormones and high hopes of how I want things to be. And that dichotomy causes me fits. But I ended up choosing the three topics I did—praising God, keeping a thankful heart, and hanging in there when God hurts my feelings—because they have helped me most in my basic, everyday struggles.

I do okay avoiding what I deem the "big sins"—adultery, murder, and stealing. It's the more subtle sins of the mind and heart that trip me up. Of course, all sin is big sin because it separates me from God. Did you know Satan's very name means "one who casts something between two to cause a separation"? And his schemes are pinpointed right at my weaknesses.

I want to keep a great attitude, keep my schedule manageable, keep my emotions under control, and love those people closest to me like crazy. Then I pull a load of laundry out of the dryer with red splotches all over every piece of my oldest daughter's favorite clothing.

Red lipstick left in the pocket of a jacket thrown into the wash at the last minute by her little sister. Mercy.

Suddenly, you'd never know I have been to church the past five Sundays in a row. My flesh just rises up, ushers my good Bible study self right out of the laundry room, and strips from my mind every verse on patience I've ever memorized. I default to acting like a crazy woman. Crazy, I tell you. And I hate that kind of crazy. It's the kind of crazy that makes me lie awake at night and vow to do better. But then it happens again and the shame, guilt, and feelings of yuck make me pull back from God and deem myself a failure.

If you've ever been there, take heart. From one crazy woman to another, I can tell you there is hope. We can reset our default button, those go-to emotions that make us act crazy. Just a few shifts in perspective and some new biblical thought patterns can make a big difference. An everyday difference. Ready to start learning what to do when your uglies come out, when you lose your groove, and when God hurts your feelings? Me too.

Chapter 10

WHEN MY UGLY COMES OUT

I couldn't even blame this one on hormones. It was just too much, happening too fast, in too condensed of a time period, with too many people determined to get on my last good nerve.

I'll give it to you in two-word snippets. And while I'm running down my list, see if any empathy starts to find its way to your heart. Because I'm convinced if there is one way all us girls are alike, it's in the reality that life ain't always so pretty.

Computer crash.	Urgent errands.
Birthday forgotten.	No time.
Starbucks closed.	Doctor appointment.
Whiny child.	Waiting room.
Stained pants.	Waiting room.
Pounds gained.	Waiting room.
Feelings hurt.	Misplaced belonging.
Tempers short.	Futile search.
Dog fleas.	Hand wringing.
Pantry ants.	Messy kitchen.
Throbbing head.	Chores undone.
Interrupted nap.	Laundry piles.
Sibling spat.	Paper piles.
Time out.	Dinner flop.
Messy car.	Early bedtime.
Gas prices.	Sheer exhaustion.

And yes, all that and more happened on my birthday. And all the girlfriends sighed a unified, "Have mercy."

I really wish I could put a godly spin on how I reacted in these situations. I would love to share how I smiled and remained calm and didn't yell at those I love and didn't pout about the forgotten birthday. I would love to be able to say I took the high road and handled everything with grace as my little halo shined.

But I'm afraid only one word describes my overall attitude: "ugly."

Since days like this are a reality, what's a girl to do? Especially a girl on a quest to live out the realities of Jesus in the midst of everyday life. Everyday life that sometimes gets quite messy, inconvenient, ill-timed, and ill-tempered, I might add.

She heads to the pantry to eat her weight in chocolate pretending she's never heard the word "calorie" before. Simultaneously she calls her girlfriend who she knows will understand her slurred words despite all the smacking. And she huffs and she puffs, just wanting to blow her whole house down.

Oh, I do know of that which I speak.

No, after my ugly meltdown I was so spent I didn't even want to head to the pantry. I didn't want to forget the word "calorie." I didn't want to call my friend.

I wanted help. Real help. Jesus help. I picked up my Bible and got honest with God. *Help me in this moment. Please, Lord, intervene in my natural-flesh response right now. Block me from acting how I feel like acting and show me how to diffuse my frustration and anger.*

There were no lightning bolts. No booming voices. No phone calls telling me of instant fixes. And there certainly was no sudden loss of appetite where chocolate was concerned. So, I waited.

From across the room I heard my computer beep, signaling an incoming email. Since it was the first thing that happened after my prayer, I decided to investigate. The email was an urgent prayer request for the family of a fellow author and blogger. She had lost her battle with cancer.

As I clicked the link to her blog, I was shocked to see her name with two dates listed below it. One was the date of her birth. The other was a date I'd written on hundreds of forms and celebrated with many a cake: my birth date ... and her going-home date.

Because a blog is like an online journal, I was able to read much about her life. Things she was thinking and feeling before she got sick. Things she was thinking and feeling after the diagnosis. There were vibrant pictures of her doing life with her loved ones, and hard photos of her in a hospital bed with loved ones singing hymns over her. All stuff that occurred during that little dash between the two dates.

THE DASH

I'm not the first person ever to be captivated by the dash between dates that mark the length of a person's life. I've seen a poem that mentions it, and I've heard my pastor preach a sermon on it. But this day, it struck me unlike any other time. A simple mark between two dates that now contained an entire lifetime.

A complete lifetime of choices that would now serve as her legacy.

As I kept reading my friend's blog, I stumbled across an entry written by her daughter. In it she told of a particularly hard day where she had grabbed the Bible and cried out to God much in the same way that I had done just minutes before. Only the Bible she grabbed was on a shelf beside her dying mother's bed. Her mother's Bible flipped open to page with a blue sticky note that cited this passage:

> Praise the LORD, O my soul; all my inmost being, praise his holy name. Praise the LORD, O my soul, and forget not all his benefits—who forgives all your sins and heals all your diseases, who redeems your life from the pit and crowns you with love and compassion, who satisfies your desires with good things so that your youth is renewed like the eagle's. (Psalm 103:1–5)

The Lord spoke through this Scripture, through this blog entry, through this daughter, through my friend and her life, and through the announcement of her death that popped into my inbox right at the moment I cried out to Him. And this passage outlined everything I needed to do in my ugly moment: *praise the Lord and remember how He forgives me, heals me, redeems me, loves me, has compassion on me, satisfies my desires in good ways, and renews my strength.*

To say I was amazed is an understatement.

I felt as if I was suddenly drinking living water from a fire hose. So many life lessons coming at me so fast. But the biggest one of all was how easy it would have been for me to miss my direct answer to prayer. I had prayed for God to help me and to intervene in my natural-flesh response. But what if I hadn't connected the dots between my prayer and this email? I suddenly realized that God is always present, always aware, always available, and always actively participating in our lives if only we'll make the choice to see Him — really see Him.

GOD IS WITH US, EVEN WHEN WE DON'T FEEL HIM

When my ugly comes out, I am so often tempted to think God leaves me. I wouldn't blame Him. Who wouldn't want to get away from someone with an ungrateful heart and a stinky attitude?

But God is too full of grace to walk away. Grace doesn't give me a free pass to act out how I feel, with no regard to His commands. Rather His grace gives me consolation in the moment, with a challenge to learn from this situation and become more mature in the future.

Grace is the sugar that helps the bitter pills of confession and repentance go down without choking. That's why the writer of Hebrews says, "Let us then approach the throne of grace with confidence, so that we may receive mercy and find grace to help us in our time of need" (Hebrews 4:16). Grace is the reason I can go to God quickly, immediately — *before* I'm cleaned up — and boldly ask for His help. In the midst of my mess, God is there.

Grace is the sugar that helps the bitter pills
of confession and repentance go down without choking.

When I am short-tempered and flat-out grumpy, I often don't feel God. But the reality is, He is with me. All I have to do to sense His presence is to acknowledge His presence, ask for His help, and make the choice to praise Him despite my feelings.

PRAISE = PRESENCE

Three of the most life-changing words in the entire Bible are "Praise the Lord." Praise is the key that releases God's character back into even the ugliest of attitudes and darkest of situations. The Bible says that God inhabits the praises of His people (Psalm 22:3 KJV). In other words, where there is praise, God's presence can be felt. And what does His presence bring with it? The fruit of His character: love, joy, peace, patience, kindness, goodness, faithfulness, gentleness, and ... cough, cough ... self-control (Galatians 5:22–23).

Satan delights in our anxiety, anger, and frustration, and would love to keep darkness drawn over our hearts and minds. He breeds within our dark ugliness all that is opposite of God's character: hate, despair, fear, impatience, rudeness, self-centeredness, self-reliance, harshness, and acting out of control.

But as soon as we praise God, Satan flees. Praise pulls back the dark curtains and breathes fresh life into a weak and weary soul.

A PRAISE REALITY CHECK

I can almost hear your thoughts ... *Oh come on, Lysa, the last thing I think about doing or feel like doing when the uglies hit is praising God.* I agree, the last thing *I* typically think about or feel like doing in difficult moments is praising God. That's why I have to make the conscious effort to do so.

Please hear my heart. I am not encouraging anyone to be fake here. I am not saying we all walk around with big ol' lipstick smiles saying:

Thank You, Lord, for this cancer.
Thank You, Lord, for this car wreck.
Thank You, Lord, for this financial blow.
Thank You, Lord, for this unexpected bill.
Thank You, Lord, for this child's temper tantrum.
Thank You, Lord, for that person talking ugly about me behind my back.

No. I'm not saying that we have to fake our way into being happy about our circumstances. That makes people in the world shake their heads and deem Christians as crazy people.

What I *am* saying is that we can praise God despite our circumstances. Praise *Him*, not our circumstances. Watch how the statements I just made gain sincerity when God is my focus rather than my circumstances:

God, circumstances change, but I praise You because You never do.
God, I praise You for never leaving me.
God, I praise You for being trustworthy.
God, I praise You that You are with me in this moment and You stand in my tomorrow as well.
God, I praise You for being the wisdom I can lean on when I have none of my own.
God, I praise You for your love and Your compassion that never fails.

This kind of praise acknowledges that while a circumstance can be hard, God is still in control. Like a friend of mine recently told me, "We must keep choosing to operate in the sovereignty of God. That's how we do things around here."

*I'm not saying that we have to fake our way
into being happy about our circumstances. That makes
people in the world shake their heads and deem
Christians as crazy people.*

I like that statement. Sovereignty means power and authority. I like saying that by praising God, I am making the choice to operate in the power and authority of God. For too long, I operated in my feelings and emotions, which got me in a heap of ugly trouble.

Praising God works. But don't just take my word for it. I challenged the women who read my blog to try praising God the next time their uglies popped out. Here's what a few of them had to say:

Bridgett: My uglies were getting out of control with my children, so I thought I would take a long bath, listen to some praise music, and come back when ugly had left the building (or at least when my husband would be home and he could deal with the kids). Unfortunately, both of my kids kept interrupting me; however, I wasn't yelling at them. My son ended up in my bedroom watching TV, so I couldn't turn the radio on. But ugly must have drowned, because I found myself laughing at the fact that I couldn't finish washing my hair because I wouldn't be able to hear the kids! God is good and I kept singing "He is mighty to save, He is mighty to save!"

Samantha: Wow. Praising God when your ugly comes out? I think I could have held a tent meeting in Target yesterday. Who says kids can't bring you closer to the Lord? Seriously, I think I'll give that a shot today.

Teresa: Many times I have prayed something like this.... Although the baby has not slept a wink and my house is a wreck; although the bank account is low and the toilet is overflowing; although my to-do list is long and my energy low, yet I *will* rejoice in the Lord, I will be joyful in God my Savior!

Though praise is not often the first or even the tenth thing we naturally think about when the uglies hit, if we keep praise in the forefront of our mind it will become easier and easier to make that choice. Just like any other discipline, practicing it over and over will help it to become more natural.

A FEW KEY QUESTIONS

Though praise is the biggest way I've found to disengage my mind, mouth, and heart from going to ugly places, I also consider five other key factors. Look over the following questions to see which of these conditions might have made you susceptible to an ugly situation recently.

Am I overly tired? Getting the proper amount of rest is not easy for busy women; however, I realize that I am not doing anybody any favors if I sacrifice my rest. Not getting enough sleep weakens my defenses and heightens my emotions.

If I sense I am overly tired, I make it a priority to schedule some rest time. Even if that means other things have to slip. I've been known to spray down some clothes with Febreze instead of washing them and letting my kids eat cereal for dinner as practical ways to fit a nap into my day.

It's that important.

Am I overcommitted? Only I can honestly answer this question. When I sign up to do something, it often sounds so good months in advance. And then the week comes to deliver and suddenly I'm in a panic. I'm wringing my hands and mentally chastising myself for ever thinking that signing up for this task was a good idea.

I've learned I must write down in my schedule the things I've signed up to do. What's more, I have to schedule preparation time. If

I sign up to bring a dish to the teachers' appreciation luncheon, it's not just that day I need to block off on my schedule. I also need to block off time to shop for and cook the food.

Have I compromised some of my healthy boundaries lately? This past summer I started feeling tense, a feeling that led to a pattern of ugly responses to my kids. When I sat back and tried to discern what was behind my behavior, I realized my kids had gotten slack about asking if they could have friends over. Suddenly, we had lots of kids around all the time — eating, sleeping, hanging out.

I want my house to be the hang-out spot for my kids and their friends. But I must maintain some healthy boundaries, or I will start to feel invaded. It's not too much to ask that my kids get my permission before asking their friends to come over. After a family meeting, in which we reestablished the boundaries, I started to feel better about the order in my home.

Is there sin in my life I'm avoiding? Sin can worm its way into our hearts and affect our minds before we even realize what's hit us. When my uglies come out, I have to get honest with myself and assess what part my sin might be playing in the situation.

Sometimes I simply go far too long without asking God to reveal what sin is tripping me up and asking for His forgiveness. There is something so freeing about honestly confessing my wrong actions, motives, and thoughts to the Lord and asking Him to show me how to keep those things out of my life.

Do I have things on my calendar to look forward to? I can get through almost anything if I see I will receive a reward for my hard work. If I know I'm going to have a particularly hectic week, I'll schedule something fun I can look forward to when all the work is over.

Sometimes it's as simple as a night when my hubby and I rent a movie for just the two of us to watch together. Or it may be dinner out with a friend. Or I might take one of my kids to the local coffee shop for a treat and one-on-one conversation. Or if finances allow, we'll go on a vacation. Whatever the "treat," having one on the schedule helps fight the uglies off.

As I said at the beginning of the chapter, life ain't always pretty. That's a given. And just because you've read this chapter doesn't mean that you'll discover a quick fix and keep your ugly from ever coming out again. But maybe now, at least, you have a glimmer of hope that it is possible to make wiser choices with your thoughts, actions, and reactions. Choices that involve getting honest with yourself and learning the power of praise, especially when the uglies come knocking.

Computers will still crash, birthdays will be forgotten, kids will whine, pants will get stained, doctors will make me wait, and laundry will pile up ... none of this will change. But I hope something inside of me has. Praise the Lord!

Chapter 11

HOW JESUS HELPS ME GET MY GROOVE BACK

Last summer I had the opportunity to travel with a team from Compassion International to Ecuador. I wanted to see firsthand the work of this missions organization because Proverbs 31 Ministries was considering a partnership with them. To be honest, I didn't want to go at first. But it didn't take me long to realize I needed Ecuador more than it needed me. I'd forgotten how to look at the blessings in my life and really see them as blessings. It's ironic that when we set out to help others, we are often the ones who receive the greatest gift.

The greatest gift I received on this particular trip came when I spent time with a woman who lives in a shanty carved into a mountainside on the outskirts of Quito. Some of the other Proverbs 31 gals and I had to climb a handmade ladder that swayed and creaked as we ascended into the dark cavern she calls home.

The floors were dirt. The walls were rock. There were two rooms—a small kitchen and a bedroom. In the kitchen was a firepit, a few shelves, and a small table. Off to one side were large broken down cardboard boxes used to repair holes in the ceiling and the walls. Off to the other side was a small cot where I soon discovered two of her five children slept.

In the bedroom were two more cots, two chests, and a rough-hewn piece of furniture that served as a dresser. She and her husband slept in one of the cots; her other three children in a cot across the room. I use the word "across" very loosely, as you could reach out and hold hands with a person in the other cot. Cots that, I might add, were meant for one person.

We listened quietly as she told us about her life. Every day she gets up at 4:30 a.m. to make breakfast over an open flame. Her husband leaves at 5:00 a.m. hoping to find work. Once he's gone, she wakes her children to get them ready for school. It is a big sacrifice to send her four daughters and one son, but she and her husband want a better life for their children, and they see education as a key component.

She spends the better part of her day walking to and from the market. There is no way to refrigerate food so what little they have must be purchased each day. Once a week, she carries her family's clothes several miles to the village washing hole. After cleaning the clothes she must make the back-breaking return journey up the mountain, carrying the now-wet and heavy loads.

When I asked her how I could specifically pray for her, she teared up. These were not tears asking for pity. These were not even tears asking for a handout. These were tears of honest concern for her family.

Through the interpreter she said, "Pray for my husband to come to know Jesus and for him to have work. And pray for me to continue to have the strength I need to serve my family."

I was amazed by this dear woman's request. I would have been tempted to pray for God to change my circumstances. Instead she prayed simply for God's provision in the midst of her circumstances. I was so challenged by her prayers and her life. Her kind disposition and peaceful presence was a far cry from my own attitude, which can become skewed when inconvenienced by life.

OH, THE THINGS I CAN COMPLAIN ABOUT!

Heaven forbid Starbucks doesn't make my coffee the right temperature. And, oh, the crying shame of having such a long list of errands. I mean, what a pain to have to drive down the street, push a cart, go through the mental strain of meal planning on the fly, come home, unload all the stuff, and then figure out what to cook from my over-flowing pantry and refrigerator.

And let's not forget the never-ending sorting, stain management, washing, drying, folding, and putting away of laundry. Putting away all those clothes in dressers that have to be dusted in rooms that have to be organized with floors that have to be vacuumed — it's just exhausting sometimes.

Yes, sometimes it's very good to get a little perspective outside my SUV-driving, brick-home-living life.

I went to Ecuador to give to the people there. But in reality they were the real givers. After I returned home, I vowed to never forget all that I'd experienced.

But then life happened. Days and weeks turned into months that eventually dulled my newfound perspective. I soon slipped right back into the my-life-should-be-comfortable-and-convenient mind-set.

On one particular day I found myself tired and grumpy and I couldn't even explain why. It was that raw, edgy attitude that had thoughts running through my head like, "If one more person asks one more thing of me, my head might start spinning so fast it'll fly right off my neck."

Pleasant, huh?

I want to be fresh for my family. I want to actually smile and say nice things. Usually this comes without trying. But this time an emotional funk had settled over me. As I typically do in times like these, I sat down with my Bible and asked God to please interrupt my feelings with His truth.

Speak to me, Jesus, I prayed. *Help me process this heavy feeling I have.*

Only one word came to me. Only one word rushed across my heart and settled into my spirit. It wasn't the word I was expecting, but I suppose it is the exact word I needed.

"Thanksgiving."

It made me chuckle because that very morning I had given a mom speech to one of my kids about being thankful. I had gone out of my way to do something kind for her and was disappointed by her lack of appreciation.

"Thanksgiving should be so engrained in our hearts that it is as natural as saying 'Bless you' when someone sneezes," I said. "You shouldn't have to remember to do it. Saying 'Thank you' and being appreciative should be the thing that rests on the end of your tongue eagerly waiting to be spoken."

Ahem.

Don't you love it when God speaks directly to you through the very things you are teaching your children?

So, yes, God had a one-word parenting speech for me too: "Thanksgiving." Unlike my attempt at brilliance with the sneezing analogy (hello, where do we moms get these things?), God's speech was short and to the point.

Anyhow, I started listing things for which I am very thankful. It felt silly, a bit elementary. I wanted some deep theological truth to chew on and ponder. I wanted a big lightning strike of revelation, an instant fix ... a ready explanation.

But here I was in this basic exercise.

And the more I verbalized what I was thankful for, the less cloudy my heart felt. I couldn't explain my feelings, and I still didn't understand them, but I think verbalizing what I was thankful for was the very thing that kept me from wallowing in pity.

I made choices despite my feelings. I made the choice to get up and do the laundry, the grocery shopping, the cooking, the errand running, the kid investing. And as I verbalized my thankfulness during each task, I started seeing the treasures wrapped within. Soon I remembered my friend in Ecuador, and all that perspective I'd gained—and then lost—started falling back into place.

Suddenly I was thankful we have running water and electricity so I could do laundry by walking across the kitchen instead of walking several miles away.

I was thankful for the blessings of towels and sheets and clothing.

I was thankful for a car that could carry me to and from the grocery store. I was thankful I had money to buy the food my family needs. I was grateful for arms strong enough to lift the bags of food from my car and legs strong enough to carry them all inside. I was thankful for a refrigerator in which to store the food.

I was very thankful for my healthy kids and for the privilege it is to hear them call me Mommy. I was thankful for the constant interruptions and busy little messes that seem to be found around each corner of motherhood.

I was thankful for my child who has disabilities because I could see that God is using even those things for good, to shape him for a very specific purpose.

I was thankful that God makes a way for us to live our lives based on truth rather than on feelings.

And I was really thankful that Weight Watchers makes little chocolate cakes that only count for one point — and that my grocery store had them in stock that day.

Oh yes, ma'am.

Thanksgiving is the very way that Jesus helps us get our groove back.

PRAISING AND THANKING

In the last chapter we learned that praise is the secret to defeating life's uglies. In this chapter, we see that thanksgiving is the secret to attitude adjustment, aka getting in a funk. The uglies cause us to lash out; an attitude funk causes us to shut down.

But take heart. We can overcome both! Praise and thanksgiving work hand in hand to remind us of our position and our promise.

OUR POSITION

We are God's people. On a personal level I should often call to mind what a privilege this is. Instead of letting my thoughts get swept up in the troubles and inconveniences of the here and now, I can choose to focus on how temporary those troubles and inconveniences are in light of eternity. The apostle Paul reminds us, "For our light and momentary troubles are achieving for us an eternal glory that far outweighs them all. So we fix our eyes not on what is seen, but on what is unseen. For what is seen is temporary, but what is unseen is eternal" (2 Corinthians 4:17 – 18).

Think how powerful it would be to have a tiny scale that weighs one's thoughts and words — those filled with praise and thanksgiving would be placed on one side, those filled with grumbling and complaining on the other. I know which side I want my words to weigh down the most. I want to make it my daily goal to live in a constant state of praising and thanking God.

Each time I get frustrated I want to say, "Yes, this circumstance is a bummer. But since I am a child of God, my position allows me to see past the circumstance and find reasons to praise God and thank Him anyway." And as the apostle Paul says, in light of eternity, aren't all things we face in daily life so very temporary? Even a year, two years, ten years — they are all but a fleeting vapor compared to the glorious, worry-free eternity that awaits us with Jesus.

OUR PROMISE

In addition to reminding us of our position, praise and thanksgiving remind us of our promise. God is faithful, and I want to live like I really believe it. Remember my friend in Ecuador? After I returned from South America, I kept my promise to pray for her. Indeed, God often brings her to my mind. But on this particular day when God was challenging me to be more thankful, I remembered her specific prayer request: that she would have continued strength to serve her family's needs.

That's when it struck me. I can't just pray and walk away. I must ask God what part, if any, He wants me to play in answering her prayer. After all, maybe this whole thanksgiving exercise wasn't supposed to end just with making me a more thankful person. Maybe this whole funky feeling—that led me to submit myself before the Lord, that led me to a mind-set of thankfulness—was supposed to be an invitation to personally participate in the faithfulness of God.

I grabbed the phone and called Compassion International, the organization with which I'd traveled to Ecuador. "A donkey!" I exclaimed. "The lady I visited needs a donkey, and I want to buy her one."

God is faithful. This is His promise. He was faithful to provide for my friend. And in that moment my heart swelled to epic proportions with sheer praise and thanksgiving.

Bad attitudes breed bad attitudes. Grumpy hearts breed more grumpy hearts. Ungratefulness breeds ungratefulness.

On the flip side, praising God breeds more reasons to praise God. Thankfulness breeds more thankfulness. And a person who daily practices both praising and thanking has a rare joy that very few people possess.

> *Bad attitudes breed bad attitudes. Grumpy hearts breed more grumpy hearts. Ungratefulness breeds ungratefulness.*

A SHIFT TO LIVING IT OUT LOUD

A person whose life is characterized by constant praise and thanksgiving despite their circumstances will shift from just verbalizing their praise and thanksgiving to living it out loud through their courageous stance for Christ. The book of Acts contains an amazing story of two people who are perfect illustrations of this point.

The story centers around Peter and John, who had just healed a crippled beggar. Healed him. Don't rush past that. A man who couldn't walk was carried to the temple gate every day to beg from passersby. A man reduced to a crumpled heap with an outstretched arm. No doubt he was dirty, stepped on, passed over, tossed aside, and ignored by most.

Then one day, two Jesus-loving men determined to be more than Bible study people noticed him and stopped. The beggar asked them for money. But Peter and John looked straight into the man's face, and Peter said, "Silver or gold I do not have, but what I have I give you. In the name of Jesus Christ of Nazareth, walk" (Acts 3:6).

And, lo and behold, the man jumped to his feet and began to walk.

As you can imagine, this caused quite a stir at the temple gate. Some bystanders were astonished. Others were greatly disturbed, especially when Peter and John told everyone that the power that allowed them to heal the beggar came straight from the resurrected Jesus.

The priests and the Sadducees, many of whom took part in Jesus' arrest and crucifixion, were outraged. They had Peter and John thrown in jail. Yet, despite their opposition, "many who heard the message believed, and the number of men grew to about five thousand" (Acts 4:4).

Then the Scriptures reveal a verse so penetrating I can hardly get it out of my mind. "When they [the priests and Sadducess] saw the courage of Peter and John and realized they were unschooled, ordinary men, they were astonished and they took note that these men had been with Jesus" (Acts 4:13).

I was forced to pause. To step back from my life. To do a little reflecting and soul searching.

What is the overflow in my life? Is it a frustrated attitude or grumbling? Or is it praise and thanksgiving? During the course of my ordinary days, do people ever see my reaction to situations and take note that I have been with Jesus?

Peter and John went on to say, "We cannot help speaking about what we have seen and heard" (Acts 4:20).

Now, make no mistake, this was a process for Peter and John just like it will be for us. Lest we forget, a few chapters back in the Bible, all of the disciples let Jesus down to some degree, and Peter denied he even knew Jesus.

But after they encountered the resurrected Jesus, all their doubts were swept away. The disciples exclaimed, "We have seen the Lord!" (John 20:25), and the glorious courage instilled in their hearts filled them to overflowing with praise, thanksgiving, and a promise to carry Jesus' message to the ends of the earth.

Peter and John were so confident in both their position as children of God and in the promise of His faithfulness that praise and thanksgiving became their way of life. Their postresurrection circumstances were never easy, often dangerous. They were inconvenienced and threatened in ways I can't even fathom. And yet their response was to boldly proclaim from their praise-filled, thankful hearts, "We cannot help speaking about what we have seen and heard." It was the overflow of their lives, and it became the routine of their lives.

Believe it or not, that leads us straight back to the theme of this chapter, "How Jesus helps me get my groove back." Do you know what one of the definitions of the word "groove" is? "A fixed routine."

What is the fixed routine or natural inclination of our heart? Is it thanksgiving and praise as we see and count the blessings of our life? Or is it grumbling and complaining because we see our blessings as constant burdens to bear? Oh, how I feel challenged by this! How I long to be like the apostles who were so consumed with thanksgiving that people took note they'd been with Jesus. God's truth was alive, active, and readily visible in their lives. How might this become a reality for us as well?

How I long to be like the apostles who were so consumed with thanksgiving that people took note they'd been with Jesus.

Whether we are a woman in Ecuador guiding a donkey up the mountain or a woman in America driving carpools and running errands, may the fixed routine of our life be praise, thanksgiving, and overflowing evidence of the presence of Jesus. Is this easy? No ma'am. Will we be challenged to slip back into letting the fixed routine of our life be grumbling and complaining? Possibly. So, let's make sure we intentionally verbalize our thanksgiving to God every day. Remember, thankfulness breeds thankfulness. The more we practice it, the more we'll live thanksgiving out loud. And the more we live it out loud, the more thanksgiving will become the natural groove of our heart.

Chapter 12

WHEN GOD HURTS MY FEELINGS

I don't know another way to say this, so I'll just shoot straight. Sometimes God hurts my feelings. Now, hear me out. I don't mean this in an irreverent way. I very much know my place, and I very much have a holy reverence for God. But tiptoeing around my gut reactions and pretending to be just fine-fine-fine with everything that comes my way doesn't pave an authentic connection between my heart and God's. So, I'm honest in my conversations with Him because I know He can handle it.

Of course, when I'm completely honest with God, I have to prepare myself for His honest response back to me. Not that God would ever be dishonest. It's just that the bolder I am with pouring out my heart to Him, the bolder He is with His responses to me.

BOLD IS BEAUTIFUL

I like bold. And I like bold responses from God because they help me know that it is His voice speaking to me and not my own. My own thoughts tell me to curl up my pity-partying self next to a big tub of chocolate ice cream and eat until I feel better. Or to arm myself with my credit card, head to Target, and throw caution to the wind. Sound familiar?

Though God has been bold with me many times, the situations I remember most are those when I've been disillusioned by a life circumstance—often a conflict with another person—and have taken my frustrations to Him. I would pray for God to change the situation and just make it better. But time and time again, God wanted me to learn how to look at things from His vantage point rather than my own self-centered perspective.

The bolder I am with pouring out my heart to God, the bolder He is with His responses to me.

A few years ago I had an experience that hurt so deeply I ran straight to God with a whole bucket-load of honest reactions. I had been given the chance to work on a project I'd dreamed of doing. Years of hard work had paved the way for this opportunity. Everything was all set. And then I got the call.

Cancelled.

Not the project. No, it would go on. But *my* part in the project was cancelled. I could not for the life of me figure out what had gone wrong. Had I done something that caused them to doubt me?

None of it made sense until months later when another woman who had been considered for the project called me. She confessed to having a conversation with one of the major decision makers in which she painted me in a not-so-pleasant light. She felt horrible about it now and wanted to ask for my forgiveness.

I wanted to give her something all right, but it surely wasn't forgiveness. I suppose it was gracious of her to call and admit what she'd done, but the opportunity for the project I'd longed for was long gone.

I made my mouth say the right things, but the stinging sensation in my heart soon developed into full-blown bitterness against this woman, the company who'd listened to her, even God. As in times past, I boldly communicated my anger and anguish to God. And God was bold right back. In the best kind of way. He showed me three things:

He addressed my misperceptions about the situation by help-ing me to see it from another perspective. My perception was how wrong it was for this woman to have spoken ill of me. God's perception was that He could bring good out of even this. He didn't need me to have this opportunity to further my ministry. He could easily do that in other ways. But He did need to do some work in her heart, and He used this situation to do just that.

He helped me to see how sin clouded my view and that I was refusing to acknowledge my part. If I were really honest, the thing I was so mad about was feeling as though I had I earned this oppor-tunity, that I deserved it. This opportunity was supposed to be mine.

In reality, all opportunities are gifts from God. I wanted to take credit for something that had very little to do with me in the first place. I had misplaced notions of where this opportunity had come from and Who was really responsible for creating it.

He showed me my stubbornness and my refusal to extend grace in my effort to prove I was right. The other woman was wrong in what she did. But did that disqualify her from my forgiveness? The rub was that I wanted her to hurt as badly as I did. What if God took that stance with me every time I fell short?

I am a person who desperately needs grace; therefore, I must freely give it. I didn't need to prove I was right and withhold my forgiveness to punish her. God was dealing with her about what she'd done. My responsibility was to extend grace and make the choice to move on.

I still can't say that I completely understand why this experience happened. And while I'd like to tie the story up in a nice little bow and show you the gift of a better and bigger opportunity that came on the other side, I can't. But I *can* say I learned through this loss how ugly jealousy can be. And you better believe this situation causes me to pause each time jealousy invites me to entertain her. And that is a bold, beautiful gift.

DEEP GRIEF

Sometimes when hurts and disappointments come, they cause a temporary panic that rises and falls in a mini-tidal wave. Like the event I just shared. The hurt feelings escalated, crested with some hand-wringing and mind-racing, and then slowly ebbed away. In the end, I could see how God grew me through it, and I wound up being thankful for that growth.

But other times the hurt comes in the form of a loss that cuts into your heart so viciously it forever redefines who you are and how you think. It's what I call deep grief. The kind that strains against everything you've ever believed. So much so you wonder how the promises that seemed so real on those thin Bible pages yesterday could ever possibly stand up under the weight of your enormous sadness today.

I once stood beside a casket far too small to accept—the one containing my baby sister, Haley. Pink roses draped everywhere. And I watched my mom as she lay across the casket, refusing to let go. How could she? Part of her heart was sealed within that casket, so quiet and still.

Just days ago we were laughing and doing everyday things, assuming that all of our lives stretched before us in spans of many, many years. And then suddenly everything stopped. I was paralyzed.

In the flurry of funeral plans and the memorial service, we operated on automatic. People were everywhere. Soft chatter filled the gaps that our stunned silence could not. And enough food was brought in to feed the whole neighborhood.

But eventually people went back to their own lives. The soft chatter dissipated. The food stopped coming. And we were forced to carry on. Except that our deep grief was still wrapped about us, strangling our throats and setting our feet in thick mud.

I remember I tried to go to McDonald's to order a Happy Meal. But I couldn't. I sat in the drive-thru with the speaker spouting words at me I couldn't process. The woman in the speaker kept asking if she could take my order.

Yeah, I had an order. Take away my bloodshot eyes. Take away my desire to hurt the doctors who couldn't save my sister. Take away my anger toward God. And then take away my guilt for being the one who lived. I'll take all that with no onions and extra ketchup, please.

I drove away sobbing. How dare they offer Happy Meals. No one should be happy today. Or tomorrow. Or next year.

This is the reality of deep grief.

I've already mentioned how I walked away from God at that time. That is how many people process loss. But I've even seen people walk away from God over situations like the first one I shared in this chapter. Disillusionment can break people.

It's understandable, really. We are told from an early age that God can do anything, and we've read the stories about Jesus helping people. But how do we process such beliefs in the face of loss? Whether the loss of an opportunity, the loss of a relationship, the loss of one's health, or the loss of a loved one, loss of any kind hurts.

Trying to come to grips with the fact God could have prevented this grief but didn't is a bit like trying to catch the wind and turn it into something visible. It's an answer we could chase our whole lives and never get. And sometimes this chase just simply wears people out. They turn and walk away, whispering, "I tried, God, but You just didn't work for me. You hurt my feelings and I don't want anything to do with You anymore."

ASKING THE RIGHT QUESTION

Looking back on my chase after the loss of my sister, I can see the reason the answer seemed so elusive. I was asking the wrong question. I was asking *why*. Why did this happen? Why didn't You stop this, God? Why were my prayers not answered? Why?

Asking why is perfectly normal. Asking why isn't unspiritual. However, if asking this question pushes us farther from God rather than drawing us closer to Him, it is the wrong question.

In most situations, nothing positive can come from whatever answer there might be to a why question. If God gave us His reason why, we would judge Him. And His reasons, from our limited perspective, would always fall short. That's because our flat human perceptions simply can't process God's multidimensional, eternal reasons. God describes it this way: "'For my thoughts are not your thoughts, neither are your ways my ways,' declares the LORD. 'As the heavens are higher than the earth, so are my ways higher than your ways and my thoughts than your thoughts'" (Isaiah 55:8–9). We can't see the full scope of the situation like God can; therefore, we must acknowledge that His thoughts are more complete and that He is more capable of accurately discerning what is best in every circumstance.

Asking why isn't unspiritual. However, if asking this question pushes us farther from God rather than drawing us closer to Him, it is the wrong question.

In the case of losing a loved one, love skews even the most rational parts of us. Our love for the person we lost would never allow God's reasons to make us feel any better or to understand any more fully. We would still feel as though God had made a terrible mistake.

So, if asking the why question doesn't offer hope, what will? The *what* question. In other words: Now that this has happened, *what* am I supposed to do with it?

Good can come from any loss if we make the choice not to resist the birthing process required to bring this good to life.

Good did eventually come from Haley's death. I can stand here twenty years later and assure you of that. And I can assure you that good still comes in small, unexpected ways. Just last week my mom and I had the most amazing conversation we've ever had about Haley's death. We both experienced a spiritual breakthrough I thought might never come.

I shared with my mom that Psalm 139:16 tells us every person has a certain number of days assigned to them: "All the days ordained for me were written in your book before one of them came to be." Nothing we do or don't do can add to or take from that number. She was finally able to let go of a lot of questions and guilt surrounding the medical problems that eventually caused Haley's death. And I was able to see the beauty of God reaching my mom in a new way. But that conversation was twenty years in the making.

It Takes Time

It takes time. Even when you love God and believe in His promises. Even when you know without a doubt that you will see your loved one again. Even when you know hope is still there.

It takes time.

It takes wading through an ocean of tears.

It takes finding a possession of your loved one that you thought was lost and realizing God did that just to comfort you. It takes discovering one day that the sun still shines. It takes being caught off guard when you catch yourself smiling, only to realize it's okay.

It takes prayer. It takes making the decision to stop asking for answers and start asking for perspective. It takes telling people to please not avoid saying her name — you want to hear it, over and over and over again.

Then one day you take off the blanket of deep grief. You fold it neatly and tuck it away. You no longer hate it or resist it. For underneath it wondrous things have happened.

The why questions have been replaced with truths from God's Word. Verses that stung to read at first have now become the very lifeline you cling to. God's presence has fallen softly upon you and helped you see that good can come and will come in you and through you.

Yes, in time things have happened. Wondrous things. Things that could have only come about because divine hope still intersects with our broken world. The secret is letting God's Word get into you to achieve the purpose He intends.

Then you can lift up your despair, your doubts and questions, your feelings of being hurt by God. And with open hands held high, you let the wind blow them all away.

And, finally, you will see years stretching before you once again. Hope stretching before you again. New perspectives even when others hurt you again. Possibility stretching before you again. And more honest conversations with God stretching before you again.

Part 5

BECOMING MORE THAN A GOOD BIBLE STUDY GIRL

IN MY THOUGHTS

I can think of 1,642 things I'd rather do than laundry. But lest my family and I wear stinky clothes, it's a must. Recently, I'd fallen terribly behind with this dreaded chore, and I was determined to catch up all in one day. I was clicking right along until the dryer stopped me short.

I'd thrown in a load, set the timer, and walked away—knowing it'd be dry in an hour or so. Twenty minutes later, a strange beep emerged from the laundry room.

I walked in, looked at the flashing light on the top of the dryer, and discovered the lint filter was dangerously full. As I retrieved the overflowing lint from the filter, a horrifying thought occurred to me. What might have happened had the dryer not had a shut-off switch when the lint filter was full? I've known several people whose homes burned to the ground as a result of a fire in their dryer. Scary.

I cleaned out the filter and was about to reinsert it when another thought struck me: *my mind is a lot like this lint filter.* An un-cleaned-out mind can be just as dangerous as a clogged-up lint filter. A stuck thought slows things down; prevents fresh, pure winds from blowing freely; and, left alone, can become all-consuming.

I started thinking about some thoughts that have gotten stuck in my mind's filter lately. Especially paralyzing are the nagging questions when I wonder, *Could my husband ever have an affair?* I know it's an irrational fear, rooted in my father's betrayal. Art has given me every reason in the world to feel secure and safe in our relationship, but if I'm not careful, irrational fears can start to affect the way I treat him.

Just that day I'd gotten an alarming call from a friend who'd been blindsided by her husband's affair. I let my fearful thoughts run rampant. I called Art and couldn't reach him. More mind reeling. By the time I talked with him a few hours later, I was snappy and emotional, hints of distrust in my tone.

Alone, misguided thoughts seem benign. But piled on top of one another, they clog up everything. Suddenly my attitude grows a little sour, my heart a little cold, my desire to be around others diminishes, and my prayers become canned obligatory statements.

I need a fresh wind. I need to let God peel away the layers of untrue thoughts. I need an encounter with Him, His regular reminders. The majestic still visits us in the midst of our mundane, ordinary, everyday lives.

So let God visit you in this section as together we learn how to break free from negative, self-distracting patterns of thinking; find a new filter for all our thoughts; and move past wishful thinking for a deeper walk with God to the real thing.

Chapter 13

WHAT DO I DO
WHEN I DON'T FEEL GOD?

The air was electric. Thousands of fans were squealing, screaming, and singing along in absolute awe of this rock star. Flashes strobed everywhere. Hands reached out, hyperextending, just trying to get his attention.

Signs were held up that proclaimed support and love. T-shirts were purchased. Lines and crowds were endured. Autographs were signed. And with great dramatic sighs, vows were made to never again wash the hand that touched his.

A fabulous time was had by all.

I was in the audience that night, amazed by the size of the arena, the volume of the cheers and applause, the sheer excitement of being in the moment. At one point all eyes keyed on a ten-year-old girl who was acknowledged by the singer and given the happy-birthday wish of a lifetime.

As I sat there and thought about how exciting it must have been for that girl to get attention from this star that thousands of others craved, my mind wandered away from the concert. I remembered times when I felt so small and unnoticed — even by God. Lost in the crowd. Unable to feel God. With all the millions of people in the world, how is it really possible for God to love us and be intimately involved with our lives? Jesus. Emmanuel. He is God with us. I imagined Jesus standing up on that stage. I imagined the whole crowd fading away as He points

His finger straight up to me in the cheap seats. Little ol' insignificant me, sitting in row 116, section R, seat 24. And then He speaks straight to me, "I love you, Lysa, and I have chosen you. Can we spend some time talking about this?"

I smiled. Then the reality of the concert brought real life crashing back. To the rock star, the person sitting in row 116, section R, seat 24 is just another face in the crowd. That's all he's capable of seeing. After all, though he may seem larger than life up on that stage, the reality for the rock star is the same reality for us — he's just human. But to Jesus there is no such thing as just another face in the crowd. Somehow, to God we are all unique souls who He desires to call out, recognize, and invite into a more intimate setting.

Unlike a human star, Jesus can give such individual attention without excluding others. Every single person in the crowd could have their own individual encounter with Him. The only requirements are the *desire* to experience Him and the *belief* that it is possible. Sadly, very few people have either.

I know. I used to have the kind of relationship with God where I viewed Him as the One who makes sweeping glances over thousands of people per minute just to make sure no one is getting out of line. But the possibility of having God pause in the midst of everyday life to spend time with just me wasn't at all in my scope of possibilities.

CHOSEN

Doesn't it seem presumptuous to think God would want to notice us as individuals, to choose us, call on us by name, and converse with us one-on-one?

Maybe the answer to this question is yes in human terms, but no in biblical terms. But before we talk about the biblical terms, let's clear some things up about the human terms. In human terms, the word "chosen" sends my mind reeling back to the days of playground kickball.

At my school, it was well known who you did want and who you didn't want on your kickball team. To be part of the elite kickball group, you had to have one of two things going for you: either a proven track record in past kickball games or proven physical prowess. You could be forgiven your lack of kickball skills if you had done well on the annual Presidential Fitness Award program, thus showing some kind of kickball potential.

As a side note, I must comment on the Presidential Fitness Award program. Why the White House had to get involved with elementary aged kids and their fitness goals, I will never have a clue. Every spring the day of this test struck a chord of dread unmatched by any other school day, except for the one when the girls were supposed to ask the boys to the Sadie Hawkins dance. But that's a story for another day.

Anyhow, my elementary school experience dates to the Jimmy Carter era. I think Jimmy could have been plenty busy with Strategic Arms Limitations Talks and Panama Canal treaties. But somehow he also had time to worry about whether or not fourth graders could do push-ups, pull-ups, and run a mile without passing out.

Back then, telling me to run a mile was like asking me to run all the way from Florida to California. I came from a family who thought it necessary to sweat only if you were lying out in the sun. And a pull-up? A push-up? I didn't even know arms had muscles. I thought those were strange things you found in other people's *legs*. So I was a sore disappointment to Jimmy, his program, and my PE teacher.

Needless to say, when it came time for the two team captains to choose kickball teammates, I didn't fare so well. I hated that feeling of everyone else getting picked while I was passed over round after round. Finally, there was no choice but to take one of the leftover players, so my name was called. I'd hang my head and kick the dirt all the way over to stand with my team. "Chosen" was not at all a word I would have used to describe myself.

When I first heard the word "chosen" in relation to God's feelings toward me, I couldn't process it. In human terms, it seemed quite presumptuous to think God would pause to pay attention to me. My earthly daddy never did. My kickball teammates certainly didn't. It seemed quite upside down to think that a girl the world ignored and passed over would actually be handpicked, on purpose, by God.

When I first heard the word "chosen" in relation to God's feelings toward me, I couldn't process it. In human terms, it seemed quite presumptuous to think God would pause to pay attention to me.

Yet the Bible is full of reassurances that this is exactly the way God wants us to process life. Consider these words from the apostle Paul: "Therefore, as God's *chosen* people, holy and dearly loved, clothe yourselves with compassion, kindness, humility, gentleness and patience" (Colossians 3:12, emphasis added). The psalmist writes, "Who, then, is the man that fears the LORD? He will instruct him in the way *chosen* for him" (Psalm 25:12, emphasis added). And Jesus says, "If you belonged to the world, it would love you as its own. As it is, you do not belong to the world, but I have *chosen* you out of the world" (John 15:19, emphasis added). Noticed. Picked for a specific reason—a specific purpose. Treasured. Loved. Isn't that the heart cry of every human? It's a heart cry that only Jesus can completely satisfy.

I am—and you are—a chosen person, with a chosen way, who has been handpicked by God on purpose to live a chosen life, set apart in this world. But please don't mistake this as an exclusive country-club-type membership. No, every person can stand on this truth, no matter their race, background, or past. If you proclaim Jesus Christ, the Son of God, as your Lord and Savior, this is your chosen reality.

THE PROBLEM ... AND THE SOLUTION

The problem is, we have been trained to process life based on the way we feel. We think we must feel love for love to exist. We think we must feel wanted to truly be chosen. We think we must feel God's presence for Him to really be close. But God never meant for us to feel our way to Him.

God wants us to stand on the absolute truth that He is with us no matter how our feelings may betray that reality. When I process life through my feelings, I am left deceived and disillusioned. When I process life through God's truth, I am divinely comforted by His love and made confident in His calling on my life.

I used to say I didn't feel close to God, and therefore, God must not be close to me. Now, I say: *God is close, and if I choose to be close back, He'll rearrange my feelings.* In other words, I need to make an intentional choice with my head, knowing that my heart will eventually follow.

That's how this anti-sweat, non-chosen kickball player, couch-potato girl finally got into exercising. And let me assure you my heart was not at all into it! Not even the tiniest bit. And let me further assure you that I'm not in it for speed and would still not impress Jimmy or qualify for his Presidential Fitness Award.

But none of that is the point. The point is, I made a choice despite my feelings, and I achieved victory.

One day I chose to get up off the couch, bought some running shoes, and set out to run from my mailbox to that of my neighbor. The next day, I ran a little farther. A few days after that, farther still. And I've been making the choice to run ever since. I stay motivated because running keeps me in shape, and I love how I feel afterward, both emotionally and physically. But I'll admit there are still days when I'd rather just pull the covers over my head and stay in bed.

I was sharing this with a friend one day, and she seemed shocked by my confession that running is still a choice I have to make. She admitted to thinking that each morning I just hop out of bed eager to strap on my running shoes and hit the open road. She thought running was simply effortless for me.

Our conversation made me laugh. Some days my runs are easier, but never are they effortless. Each mile—each and every step—is a choice. And there is still plenty of heavy breathing and the need to stop and walk every now and then.

But do you want to know a little secret? I've never regretted running. I've regretted *not* running. I can honestly say every single minute I spend running is time well spent.

The same can be said for my time with the Lord. Some days it's as natural as having a face-to-face conversation with a friend. I just open my Bible and the revelations are rich, the dialog flows, and the encouragement I receive sends my soul soaring.

Other days, it's more of an effort. When I feel things are awkward or blocked between me and the Lord, I ask Him why and then sit quietly waiting for some revelation to brush across the corners of my mind. Sometimes it's unconfessed sin. Sometimes it's a bad attitude I've been harboring. Sometimes it's my to-do list tempting me to cut my quiet time short.

Whatever is holding me back, there is beauty in pausing for the One I should seek over all else. This is how the Bible describes it: "One thing I ask of the LORD, this is what I seek: that I may dwell in the house of the LORD all the days of my life, to gaze upon the beauty of the LORD and to seek him in his temple" (Psalm 27:4). Pausing with God, waiting for Him to reveal something to me, isn't always easy—but it is absolutely essential for my soul's well-being. Just as my physical body needs food for energy and life, so my soul needs time with the Lord for sustenance as well.

One thing I can say for sure, I never walk away from spending time with the Lord feeling less close than when we started. I don't stop spending time with the Lord until I've learned or received something from Him; therefore, every moment spent with the Lord is time well spent.

The psalmist writes, "Those who know your name will trust in you, for you, LORD, have never forsaken those who seek you" (Psalm 9:10). To seek means "to go to, to attempt, or to ask for." Shouldn't this be how we pursue God? We go to Him. We give our greatest, undivided attempts to get to know Him. We ask for His revelation and His help. We keep making the choice to do it over and over again. And if we do this, God promises He will not leave us empty-handed or empty-hearted.

Wait, don't rush past that last sentence. If we do this, if we make the choice to ask for God's revelation and help, *He will not leave us empty-handed or empty-hearted*. Let that truth sink deep into your thoughts. It's a truth that will transform your approach to your everyday life, if you let it.

If we make the choice to ask for God's revelation and help, He will not leave us empty-handed or empty-hearted.

And since these times with God are so key, why not record them in some way? I know, I know, I can hear you objecting. I used to be emotionally allergic to journaling as well. For some, journaling seems very unrealistic. I have a friend who has boxes full of daily journals. When she told me this, her commitment overwhelmed me. I was resistant and hesitant for fear of it being one more thing I started and couldn't stick with.

However, I've found recording my times and revelations with God is completely refreshing. I don't use a paper journal, like my friend. I use my daily blog[8] as a place to record and dialog with others about the things God teaches me and my many adventures with experiencing Him.

However you feel most comfortable, I want to encourage you to do some type of journaling. Some days your quiet time entry might be just three heartfelt words: "Lord, help me!" Other days you may have a lot more to write. Give yourself permission to just let your thoughts flow without getting caught up in the mechanics. Even if it is only random phrases, pieces of verses, or stream-of-consciousness prayers, it is beautiful to capture your time with God. It's your acknowledgment that He is close, no matter how you feel.

I'm a visual learner and always like an example of something before I try to do it myself. So I've included one of the longer entries from my blog. But, before you read it, let me assure you I have plenty of those "Help me, Jesus" days as well.

A SAMPLE FROM MY OWN QUIET TIME JOURNAL

It is very early in the morning. Not many people are stirring yet.

Though my body begged me just to roll over and go back to sleep, my soul was stirring to get up and go sit with Jesus.

Though I can't physically see Him, I know He is present.

I decide to open up my Bible to the Psalms and use the verses I read as prayers to start my day. And the more I pray those verses out loud, the less I hear all the nagging things of the world. A beautiful melody of truth starts to rise up and suddenly my worries fade in the light of God's truth.

His perspective on things that are troubling me starts to overshadow my anxiety. Like shade on a hot summer's day, I feel relief in His presence.

I know that He is preparing me for what I will need throughout this day. He is already standing in every minute of my day and He sees what I will face. He's equipping me to be able to handle what is ahead of me with His gentle boldness, quiet strength, and loving grace.

God instructs me, "Open wide your mouth and I will fill it" (Psalm 81:10). He will give me what to say today. What to say in happy moments.

What to say in aggravating moments. What to say in moments where I feel insecure and what to say when I feel completely confident. What to say in disappointing moments. What to say in response to questions. He also reminds me that sometimes it is good to keep my mouth closed and say nothing at all.

All the words that rumble about in my brain and those that will proceed out of my mouth, Lord, You be the author of those.

I read, "How lovely is your dwelling place, O LORD Almighty!" (Psalm 84:1). So I ask God to dwell in me richly. I want Him to be what radiates about me. I want Him to be my pretty today. Not my hair. Not my outfit. Not my efforts of adornment. But simply Him and His spirit dancing invisibly about me . . . shifting a wrong attitude, guarding my words, and whispering constant truths into my heart.

These words leap off the page: "Teach me your way, O LORD, and I will walk in your truth; give me an undivided heart" (Psalm 86:11). In response, I ask the Lord to give me the gift of an undivided heart. I use all He gave me in my devotion time with Him to direct my prayer and clearly proclaim how near I know He is.

> *Lord, may nothing separate me from You today. Teach me how to choose only Your way today so that each step will lead me closer to You. Help me walk by the truth today and not my feelings.*
>
> *Help me to keep my heart pure and undivided. Protect me from my own careless thoughts, words, and actions. And keep me from being distracted by MY wants, MY desires, MY thoughts on how things should be.*
>
> *Help me to embrace what comes my way as an opportunity . . . rather than a personal inconvenience.*
>
> *And finally, help me to rest in the truth of Psalm 86:13, "Great is your love toward me."*
>
> *You already see all the many ways I will surely fall short and mess up. But right now, I consciously tuck Your whisper of*

absolute love for me into the deepest part of my heart. I recognize
Your love for me is not based on my performance. You love me
warts and all.

Have mercy, that's amazing.

But what's most amazing is that the God of the universe,
the Savior of the world, would desire a few minutes with me this
morning. Lord, help me to forever remember what a gift it is to
sit with You like this.

AND THEN THE STAGE LIGHTS DIMMED

So, back to that concert when Jesus gave me the visual of Him calling out to me and choosing me. I learned something profound that night. God made each of us with a vulnerable place inside our souls—a desire to be wanted, loved, and chosen above all others. I think that's what ultimately drives people on both sides of an arena-filled stage. The person on stage is looking to have this vulnerable place filled by the screaming crowd. The screaming crowd somehow thinks this famous person has it all figured out; if only they can just get close, some of that fulfillment will surely rub off on them.

All the while Jesus stands off to the side and wonders if anyone realizes He's the One our souls long for ... not the fame ... not the attention of the famous ... and not the millions of other things we'll spend our lives thinking we must have.

The answer to our deepest desires is not the seemingly perfect life ... not the most romantic husband ... not the smartest and most well-behaved kids ... not the bigger house ... not the better job ... not the awards and recognition of people ... not in trying to feel our way to God.

It's making the choice to recognize God is close. Whether we're at a big concert, on a playground in the middle of a sorry kickball game, running the streets of our neighborhood, or sitting in a chair in our den—God is there. Loving. Assuring. Teaching. Calling. Choosing to spend time with us.

Becoming more than a good Bible study girl means never settling for needing to feel our way to God or to limit our experience of Him to those few minutes we call our quiet time. It's being able to sit in the noise of the arena of life with every worldly distraction imaginable bombarding you and suddenly thinking of Him — talking with Him, smiling with Him, and realizing that every longing you've ever had in life to be more than just the girl in row 116, section R, seat 24 is already filled. By Him. The One who chooses you.

Chapter 14

LEARNING TO SIMPLY LIKE ME

D o you like yourself? It's an awkward question, really. For me, answering it requires a little road trip past some of life's most significant mile markers.

There is one person who has done more life with me than almost any other. She was the one who ate my mud pies fresh out of the Easy Bake oven and who was naïve enough to clean my bedroom for a whole penny.

She also was the one who saved every penny, nickel, dime, and dollar she ever got while I spent anything that came my way quicker than you could say "on sale." She kept her personal bank account inside a shoe box vault underneath her bed and would taunt me with how rich she was every time I complained of being broke.

I beat her to braces by a couple of years. She took great delight in thinking of all kinds of edifying names to call me. And being more mature, I retaliated with comments about her four eyes and home-permed hair. Those were frightening years for the both of us.

We shared the same mom. The same dad. The same broken home. The same heartbreak. And shared love for a toy poodle named Biscuit. Bless that dog's heart. I'm not sure it ever got to do normal dog things like chase cars and balls. I only remember it spending years as a make-do baby doll, much to the joy of two little girls longing for normalcy when we played house.

She was getting ready for her eighth-grade banquet when I was getting ready for my senior prom. She wore a light pink dress. I wore a black dress. Sadly, her friend had just broken out with chicken pox, but the two of us spent hours assuring this girl that nobody would notice, thanks to an entire tube of flesh-toned makeup we used to cover the spots. By the time they were ready to go, I was astonished by this brief time of bonding we'd shared. I think it was the first sign of hope that we wouldn't hate each other forever.

We're different in most every way you can imagine. She is very organized; I like to think of my piles as signs of creativity. She remains a size four even after birthing three children; I will never wear a size four. She does not exercise; I sweat my life away five days a week. Quite the unfair commentary on the mysteries of genetics and who gets what metabolism.

Not that there is an ounce of jealousy on my part. I'm just stating the facts.

The truest fact of all is that I feel blessed for getting to do life with my sister, Angee, for almost four decades now.

And, yes, we both have names that we've spent our lives spelling for people who look at us like we should have grown out of that middle-school phase of cutesy name spellings years ago. Only mine is in fact spelled L-Y-S-A on my birth certificate.

On the one hand, it's exciting to have a name spelled all crazylike because it makes you feel slightly cool. On the other hand, it's a bummer because no mass-produced tacky nameplate rack ever has your name.

So, while all the other pink Huffy bikes in my neighborhood had a rockin' nameplate, I had a bubble lettered homemade sign on my knock-off Huffy. Nothing speaks cool like an index card surrounded by duct tape flapping in the breeze as you blaze the trails of childhood.

One day in the grocery store I almost swallowed my tongue with the gasp I let out in the cleaning products aisle. All the cans of cleanser were turned so that all I could see was a massive row of L-Y-S's — and I thought I'd died and gone to personalized nameplate heaven. But just as I was making plans to strap one of those cans to the back of my bike, I saw the O-L on the end, making the word "Lysol" and not "Lysa."

I think of this incident every time I see a can of Lysol, I kid you not. My childhood memories are full of the finer things of life—like cleaning products and soap opera characters. Which brings me to the reason my name is spelled crazy in the first place.

It has something to do with my mama liking a soap opera character's name but not liking this character's character. So she changed the spelling and hoped for the best with the character I would eventually develop. And if you can write three sentences in a row using the word "character" any more than I just have, you should totally win a prize.

Anyhow, I think Angee felt bad that I always had to explain the spelling of my name; so she joined in the game, and it all stuck. Eventually I learned to appreciate the uniqueness of my name and have grown to like it.

On a bigger scale, I have had to learn to appreciate my own uniqueness and, over time, have grown to like myself. I have had to learn to embrace all that makes me, me. Some things are fun and good; others are extremely difficult and painful. Somehow Jesus has used it all.

AVOID SELF-DISTRACTION

If you want to ignite a heated debate among Christians, ask this question: "Is it Christian to say you like yourself?"

Some say that the admonition to "love your neighbor as yourself" (Matthew 22:39) requires us to love ourselves so we can love others. Others quickly counteract with Matthew 16:24–26 which says, "Then Jesus said to his disciples, 'If anyone would come after me, he must deny himself and take up his cross and follow me. For whoever wants to save his life will lose it, but whoever loses his life for me will find it. What good will it be for a man if he gains the whole world, yet forfeits his soul? Or what can a man give in exchange for his soul?'"

Instead of trying to balance the truths in these Scriptures, I'd like to get to the message behind both of them. The real point isn't to focus on ourselves at all. Instead, our time is better spent learning how to make peace with who we are so that feelings of insecurity don't become a distraction to living our faith out loud.

And believe me, I've been one of those women so distracted by myself that I was rendered ineffective for the cause of Christ. Becoming more than a good Bible study girl requires a heart free of the entanglements of self-distracting thoughts.

According to the book of Hebrews, we must "throw off everything that hinders and the sin that so easily entangles" (Hebrews 12:1). To be hindered means "to be delayed, interrupted, or to have difficulty."[9] To be entangled means "to be confused, perplexed or ensnarled."[10] When we are distracted by our own thoughts of not liking ourselves, we are hindered and entangled in the truest sense.

But I love that the writer of Hebrews doesn't just present the problem without offering a solution. The greatest thing we can do when we face feelings of insecurity is to "fix our eyes on Jesus, the author and perfecter of our faith" (Hebrews 12:2).

Satan would love for us to pick ourselves apart, to obsess on the negative. When we do, we become hyper self-focused and take our eyes off of Jesus and the mission set before us. Many of us spend years trying to hide or fix what we perceive as personal flaws.

Jesus would love for us to see ourselves as a package deal of unique qualities that He — the author and perfecter of our faith — saw as necessary for the life He's calling us to live.

---

*Jesus would love for us to see ourselves as
a package deal of unique qualities.*

Think of something about yourself that you have perceived as less than appealing. Now, turn your focus from seeing this as a negative thing to something that Jesus might turn completely around and use for good. Whether it's a sinful habit or some quality about yourself that makes you feel insecure, Jesus can take everything surrendered to Him and turn it around for good. Everything.

AVOID PAST DISTRACTIONS

In chapter 1 I briefly mentioned my abortion. I have to say that of all the things that happened to me as a child, and all the hurt I endured, nothing made me more undone than my abortion. When the people at the abortion clinic took my child, they took part of my heart as well. I walked around in a zombielike state for many, many months, a growing hatred for myself at the root of my pain and confusion.

Up until that point, the things that brought hurt in my life were caused by others. But the abortion was a choice I made myself. It seemed like the only answer at the time. The abortion clinic workers assured me that they could take care of this "problem" quickly and easily, so I would never have to think about it again. What a lie!

My thoughts were consumed with nothing else for a very long time. Remember, becoming more than a good Bible study girl requires a heart free of the entanglements of self-distracting thoughts. We can't move forward with God when our past keeps pulling us down.

Maybe there is something from your past that haunts you and constantly interrupts your thoughts. Abortion causes secret shame and hurt to millions of women. At the writing of this book, current statistics published by the Guttmacher Institute state that 35 percent of women in the United States will have an abortion by the time they are forty-five years old. And tragically, 78 percent of those women have a religious affiliation.[11]

We can't move forward with God
when our past keeps pulling us down.

Even if an abortion is not in your past, few of us have escaped very deep hurts. May I offer you a lifeline of encouragement? You can find healing through Jesus Christ.

I don't say this as a quick swipe of hope across your deepest wounds. I say this as one who had the bandages pulled back from wounds that festered for years and had God's healing salve of truth poured over me.

For years I kept my secret buried deep within my heart. I was so ashamed, so horrified, so convinced that if anyone ever found out I'd had an abortion, I'd be rejected by all my church friends and deemed a woman unfit to serve God.

I suffered in silence wrapped in a cloak of shame.

Going to church was incredibly hard during those years. I was convinced I was the only Christian woman who'd ever had an abortion. Never did I hear another Christian woman share this as a part of her testimony or anyone speak of the hope and grace Jesus provides to those of us who were suffering from making that decision. I only heard well-meaning Christians debate the issue of abortion with very strong words. Their words stung, made my heart seize, and my eyes feel like they'd explode into a flood of a million tears.

Don't get me wrong, the issue of abortion is serious and we should take a strong stand against it. But we must also remember that it's more than a topic of religious and political debate. For many women within the church, it may be one of the most painful parts of their life story. One for which they want to find forgiveness and healing, but are too afraid of being judged to share their secret with anyone.

So they suffer in silence wrapped in a cloak of shame.

My complete healing came when I was finally able to turn my thoughts past my own healing to helping others in the same situation. It was terrifying to think about sharing my story with another person. But then I heard of a young girl who worked for my husband who was in a crisis pregnancy situation. She'd asked for a few days off to have an abortion. I was faced with a fierce tug of war in my spirit. I knew if she heard my story, she might make a different choice. But what would she think of me? What would others think if they found out? I knew God wanted me to talk to her; so would I trust Him or would I retreat back into my shame?

With shaking hands, I approached Sydney (not her real name), intent on extending God's comfort and compassion. Maybe I could just share a few Bible verses, such as 2 Corinthians 1:3–4, and offer to help her without making myself vulnerable. But during our time together, it became clear that she needed to hear my story. With cracking voice and tear-filled eyes, I decided to care more about her situation than keeping my secret hidden. I told her the truth of what I'd experienced and prayed she'd make a different choice than I had.

A year after that first meeting, I sat across from Sydney once again. She choked out a whispered, "Thank you," as she turned and kissed the chubby-cheeked boy in the baby carrier beside her. As soon as she spoke those two life-defining words, tears fell from both of our eyes. Hers were tears of relief. Mine were tears of redemption. Both were wrapped in the hope that God truly can take even our worst mistakes and somehow bring good from them.

God has brought me so far since that first meeting with Sydney. Now I travel to many crisis pregnancy events and tell my story in hopes of encouraging people to support their local centers. I also share my story from pulpits all across America, trusting that the many women in the audience will see that it is possible to be healed and restored from the tragic mistakes from our past.

But I can't reach everyone.

There are women in your sphere of influence who need to hear your story. Women who were once like me. Women who once could be found blazing life's trails on their pink Huffy bikes with carefree wonder and excitement. And then bad things happened, and they've never quite been able to get back on track.

Will you go? Will you share? Will you allow God to comfort you and then take that comfort to others? I think you'll find that you are the one who winds up doubly blessed.

Not only will you see God bring good from your past mistakes, but you will see another layer of your life purpose unfolding. The more we see our life's purpose unfold, the more we'll be secure in the person God has created us to be. The more we become secure in the person God has created us to be, the more we'll be able to make peace with liking who we are. The more we make peace with liking who we are, the more we will be able to untangle self-distracting thoughts. The less entangled we are, the more effective we'll be for Christ. And we'll start to see how we are becoming more than just a good Bible study girl!

Chapter 15

A GLORIOUS SENSE
OF POSSIBILITY

Last year my friend and assistant, Holly, and I were scheduled to fly to New Jersey for a speaking engagement. Super-Duper-Happy Airline delayed our flight one hour ... and then another hour. We weren't too concerned until one of the event coordinators in New Jersey called to tell us she'd just seen an alarming notice on the airline's website: our flight had been cancelled.

Cancelled.

Not delayed. No, ma'am.

Cancelled.

As Holly went to the gate agent to either confirm or deny this information, a blonde woman in her early thirties also walked up to ask about the flight status. While the agent made a phone call, Holly and the woman chatted a bit.

Moments later we were informed that our flight had indeed been cancelled and instructed to go to the baggage area to claim our luggage and then back to the check-in counter to get rescheduled.

So Holly headed down to the baggage claim area ... and I headed off to stand in the ticketing line. It was one of "those" lines. You know the kind. Impossibly long. Incredibly slow. It was a perfect situation for some serious people watching. And there were some very unhappy people — especially when we were all told there were no more flights to Newark or any nearby city. In other words, no matter how much we wanted to get to New Jersey by air, short of divine intervention, it would be impossible.

Meanwhile down in baggage claim, Holly met up with the blonde woman again before locating our luggage, loading it on a cart, and wheeling it inside a waiting elevator. Just as the elevator doors had shut almost fully, a hand flew into the small opening to stop them. It was the blonde woman—again. She told Holly that she had used her cell phone to reschedule her flight. "Call this number and ask to be rebooked on the same flight I am taking. It's a 5:45 flight that goes to Washington, D.C., and then connects to New York." Holly wrote down the flight numbers and times and barely had time to shout a brief thanks before the doors closed.

By the time Holly and I reconnected, I was starting to feel like we might be in for an all-night drive to New Jersey. But the ticket agent was incredibly helpful. He booked us on the exact flights the blonde woman said she was on, and life suddenly brightened. We could get to New York, which was only an hour from our hotel. And we could make it in time to get plenty of sleep to feel refreshed for the next day's conference.

We got our bags checked and made it through security in the nick of time. As we boarded the Washington flight, however, the gate agent informed us that New York was showing a 200-minute delay. Sigh. But when we got to D.C., no delays were posted. We ate a quick dinner and boarded the next flight, so touched at how God was answering our prayers.

It was then that Holly started looking for our blonde friend to thank her more properly. When she didn't see her in any nearby rows, she got up and walked up and down the aisle. Still no sign of her. Halfway through the flight, Holly canvassed the plane again, carefully checking each passenger. The woman had said she was booked on this exact flight. She just had to be there.

Unless? "For he will command his angels concerning you to guard you in all your ways" (Psalm 91:11).

We made it to the speaking engagement, still amazed at the practical, personal way God had intervened. He moved powerfully throughout the weekend, as many women started a relationship with Jesus and many more rededicated their lives to Him. And to think how close we'd come to not making the trip at all. I explained to the ladies that God had a big plan for them that weekend and therefore had made a way for us to get there.

It would have been easy to see the events that unfolded as a series of lucky breaks. But what a tragedy to see only flat perspectives of life. The Bible tells us, "God looks down from heaven on the sons of men to see if there are any who understand, any who seek God" (Psalm 53:2).

"Seek," as defined by the dictionary, literally means, "to go in search of, to try to find or discover, to attempt, to ask for."[12] It is a word rich with activity and a questlike attitude. To seek God means to actively look for Him and anticipate His activity in everything.

That's why a rereading of Psalm 53:2 breaks my heart. I wish the verse said, "God looks down from heaven on the sons of men to see the *many* who understand, the *many* who seek God." But the word is "any," not "many." Which gives me a clue that those who understand and seek God are a rare few.

Francis Frangipane, an author and pastor, once said, "We do not want to just give mental assent to Christian doctrine. We want to see, have contact with, and live in the experienced reality of Christ's actual presence."[13]

If I could give only one gift to every woman on this planet, it would be the gift of being able to glimpse God throughout their days — the miraculous mixed with the mundane. This would radically change the way we think, the way we process life, and certainly the degree to which we trust God. It would make us more than good Bible study girls.

So I invite each of us into the possibility of seeing God. Not His actual physical form, but rather evidence of His activity. I want us to be women who lift our eyes up to God every day and say, "Yes, God, there are some who seek You today! I understand it is possible to experience

You; therefore, I want that more than anything else. I will seek to see You, hear You, know You, and follow hard after You in every part of my day."

FROM EMOTION TO DEVOTION

One of my dear friends and fellow speaker with Proverbs 31 Ministries, Whitney Capps, caught a brand-new vision of God and her relationship with Him in a most unlikely way. Not too long ago, she climbed a forty-foot pole as part of a team-building activity. After a slow and hesistant ascent, she was nearly to the top when she began to panic about the next thing she was supposed to do—which was to stand on the top of the pole to take in the view. Of course, she was harnessed and steadied by the group below. But the pole was swaying, her resolve was waning, and her courage fading by the second.

Whitney is not a thrill seeker. Like most of us, she likes comfort, security, and safety. So, with one step left to climb, this was the inner dialog she told me she was having: *"I don't really have to go all the way. I'm exhausted and cramping. This is good enough for me. So you stand at the top of the pole. Is twelve more inches of height really going to change my perspective?"*

She could hear her team cheering her on. Her husband kept telling her to go for it—it would be worth it. She paused, weighing the options in her mind.

Here is where I sweat, just remembering what my friend did next! She gave one final push, went for standing on the top ... and fell.

So was the exercise a total failure? No, far from it. First of all, Whitney learned that day how much her relationship with God was like climbing that pole. Too many times she has stopped just shy of full-on devotion to the Lord. She realized she has little spiritual stamina, that the emotion that helped her start her journey with God would never be enough to finish. She would have to have a level of devotion she wasn't sure she had.

Have you ever felt this way? Have you ever wanted more in your relationship with God but, for fear of failing, stopped just shy of full-on devotion?

Whitney's second perspective on the pole-climbing fall is just as interesting. Maybe it will encourage you spiritually, as it does me. She said, "I'm not disappointed that I fell in the last second. I'm glad that I didn't believe the lie that 'close was close enough.' The difference between emotion and devotion may only be a few inches, but the view is dramatically different. Emotion can get you near the top, but that's about it. Only devotion lets you experience a view so grand it takes your breath away. I caught a glimpse of it before I fell. It was well worth the effort."[14]

I love Whitney's honesty in recognizing she stopped just shy of full-on devotion. Boy, can I relate! Why is it that we aren't more compelled, convinced, and concerned with pursuing God more whole-heartedly? What keeps us from it? I believe too many of us have never dared to believe the glorious possibility Jesus clearly offers when He says, "Whoever has my commands and obeys them, he is the one who loves me. He who loves me will be loved by my Father, and I too will love him and show myself to him" (John 14:21).

Isn't that mind-blowing? Jesus gives us a road map to follow that will lead us straight to great love and great revelation.

JESUS WILL SHOW HIMSELF

Before we go much further, remember that this whole part of the book is about becoming more than a good Bible study girl in our thoughts. In the past two chapters, we've covered how to break free from negative, self-distracting thoughts and how to make the reality that we are God's chosen the filter for all our thoughts. Now, in this chapter, it is crucial for us to understand how to activate our thoughts about God. By activate, I mean moving beyond wishful thinking for a deeper walk with God to really putting action to that desire.

Okay, back to John 14:21. Let's put this verse under the microscope and get to the heart of what's absolutely possible.

"Whoever ... " First, Jesus says it is possible for "whoever." Last I checked, when the word "whoever" is used, that means everybody is eligible. No matter who you are. No matter what you've done. No matter how many Bible verses you do or don't have memorized. No matter how many times you've attended church. No matter how many times you've missed church. No matter if you have an advanced degree or dropped out of high school. *Whoever* can apply for this amazing promise Jesus is offering.

"has my commands and obeys them ..." Got a Bible? That's where we find Jesus' commands. If we make a breeze through the Gospels, we'll find many passages where Jesus clearly commands us how to live the life He desires for us to live. But He sums up the most important commands in Mark 12:30–31, 'Love the Lord your God with all your heart and with all your soul and with all your mind and with all your strength.' The second is this: 'Love your neighbor as yourself.' There is no commandment greater than these."

Think about it—it's hard to lie, cheat, steal, backstab, hurt, rebel, abandon, ignore, withhold, deny, show favoritism, or do any of the other things we're told to stay away from if our thoughts are committed and dedicated to loving God and loving other people.

So let's start with these two basic commands and then move on to the more specific ones. An interesting exercise would be to survey one of the Gospels—Matthew, Mark, Luke, or John—and make a list of Jesus' commands. Then, to really start examining our heart in relationship to them. Were we aware of these commands? Are we willing to obey them? Which ones come naturally? Which will be the most difficult, and why?

Remember, life is not a sprint. If you need to park on some of these commands for a while, then do it. Ask Jesus to help you fully understand the joys of obedience. Also, ask Him how you can be a woman fully committed to obedience without slipping into a legalistic approach to life. We must always remember our goal is pursuing revelations of Him. Our focus can't be just following rules but following Jesus Himself.

"he is the one who loves me." Once we understand that this verse applies to us and tells us exactly what we should be doing, the reward follows. This person speaks God's love language. God clearly says that those who have His commands and obey them love Him. This is an amazing thought to me. The God of the universe tenderly reveals that He notices those who love Him. He wants to be loved. He who is love—who is completely satisfied, without any needs—chooses to desire our love. Oh, that we would be faithful to give back to Him a fraction of the love He lavishes on us. To do this, we must obey Him.

"He who loves me will be loved by my Father, and I too will love him and show myself to him." This person will be loved by Jesus and will experience Him personally and profoundly. Jesus will show Himself to this person. At that point of revelation, it is no longer a glorious sense of possibility to see Jesus ... it is a life-changing reality.

Now, I have to quickly insert something here. Just a few years ago the previous paragraph would have struck a chord so raw in me, I might have thrown this book across the room. I would have thought, *How dare this religious, rule-following, nutcase of an author write a paragraph that seems so exclusive! God loves all people. Jesus loves all people.*

Yes, this is true. God and Jesus love all people. But sadly, not all people love God. Not all people love Jesus.

These verses are not giving us the prerequisites for having God love us. Rather Jesus is clearly explaining to us that if we love God, if we love Jesus, we will want to obey His commands. We won't be able to help but want to obey His commands. Our love for Him will compel us. Doing so will no longer be our duty; it will be our desire. We'll follow Him not to win His love or prove how good we are. But rather to live in His love and delight in how good He is.

If we love Jesus, we will want to obey His commands.
Doing so will no longer be our duty; it will be our desire.

Have you ever let yourself dare to believe that Jesus would love to show Himself to you? Not in a physical sense, where we could see Him with our physical eyes. But rather, wouldn't it make your soul come alive like never before to see evidence of His presence constantly and consistently all around you? Interestingly, the more this happens, the more we desire to be obedient and love God the way He desires us to love Him. It is a beautiful cycle!

SEEING JESUS CHANGES US

When we see Jesus, we will be changed. Changed in the best kind of way. Jesus will no longer be an emotional figment of our thoughts, He will be so real we won't be able to be anything but completely devoted to Him. And as Whitney said, this view of life is so grand it takes your breath away and is absolutely worth pursuing.

The reason Holly and I recognized the missing lady on the plane as evidence of God's activity rather than happenstance is because we've been ruined in a good way. I can hardly go through anything in life without seeing God's hand in it. And layer upon layer of these constant experiences with God have built a very secure foundation of faith.

Of course, this raises a few obvious concerns. Am I overspiritualizing in my life? What if I don't have these experiences, or what if an experience I attribute to God isn't from Him at all? I understand these questions well. I remember being skeptical. Part of me wanted something deeper with God, but I was scared.

A larger part of me wanted God to be explainable and safe. Fitting Him in a box ensured that I ran no risk of being interrupted by Him. I just wanted to do my part (be good) and have Him do His (bless me).

It was a comfortable arrangement. But it was also the very perspective that numbed my spirit and rendered my faith ineffective.

I remember hearing my Bible friends talking freely about hearing from God and seeing Him in remarkable ways. I called them my *Bible friends* while my eyes rolled and my voice mocked their enthusiasm. I remember thinking they really did overspiritualize life and take this God thing a little too seriously.

Shortly thereafter, I was standing in the canned goods aisle at the grocery store. There must have been a special on green beans, as the cans were all out of order. Some were lying on their sides; others were twisted this way and that, French-cut string beans mixed in with the regular cuts. It was messy and chaotic. I stood there and willed God to do something miraculous with these cans, to send me a message through them. Nothing came. So I left the store mad, frustrated, and convinced God doesn't speak to regular people like me.

Looking back now, I realize I wasn't truly looking to experience God. I was looking to make God act on my command. That day in the green bean aisle, I was looking for cheap magic tricks that wowed me, not divine experiences that would change me. God isn't in the business of creating change to impress people; He is in the business of impressing on people their need to be changed. There's a big difference.

Finally God got a hold of me while reading Henry Blackaby's book *Experiencing God*[15], in which he encourages us to look for God's activity all around us. There was not even a hint of doubt in Blackaby's statement. He was absolutely certain that if we desired to see God, we would.

The prophet Isaiah writes, "Since ancient times no one has heard, no ear has perceived, no eye has seen any God besides you, who acts on behalf of those who wait for him" (Isaiah 64:4). This is the same verse the apostle Paul paraphrases in his letter to the Corinthian church, in which he speaks of a very glorious sense of possibility: "However, as it is written: 'No eye has seen, no ear has heard, no mind has conceived what God has prepared for those who love him' — *but God has revealed it to us by his Spirit*. The Spirit searches all things, even the deep things of God" (1 Corinthians 2:9–10, emphasis added).

Did you catch that? "God has revealed it to us by his Spirit. The Spirit searches all things, even the deep things of God." If we have accepted Christ as our Savior, we have God's Spirit in us. Therefore, it is possible for God's Spirit to reveal to us the deep things of God.

I have heard people who quote this verse focus on the impossibility of seeing, hearing, and conceiving what God has prepared for those who love Him. But now I see that, through the Holy Spirit, God is revealing deep and wondrous things to us *right now*. And rest assured, His preparations are not just for when we get to heaven. God has amazing things prepared for us to experience here on earth as well.

And how does this happen most often? It happens in the midst of everyday life using everyday things. Divine mixed in our mundane. It's the stuff all of Jesus' parables were made of.

There is a wonderful passage in Matthew that reveals something beautiful about this: "[Jesus] told them still another parable: 'The kingdom of heaven is like yeast that a woman took and mixed into a large amount of flour until it worked all through the dough.' Jesus spoke all these things to the crowd in parables; he did not say anything to them without using a parable. So was fulfilled what was spoken through the prophet: *'I will open my mouth in parables, I will utter things hidden since the creation of the world'*" (Matthew 13:33–35, emphasis added).

God foretold in the Old Testament that Jesus would reveal the divine (utter things hidden) using stories from everyday mundane things (parables). It has been God's plan from the very beginning to reveal Himself, His activity, and the reality of His presence to us in everyday ways.

So what do you do if you aren't currently experiencing God in this way? The Bible tells us that those with a pure heart will see God (Matthew 5:8). It doesn't say we have to be perfect or perfectly ready; it just says that we have to get to a place where our hearts purely desire to see Him — and then we will.

Tell God of your desires. Ask Him to reveal anything that may be blocking your view. And then start looking. But remember, seeing God isn't for the purpose of being wowed. It is for the purpose of changing us, growing us, and strengthening us to become more than people with mere knowledge of God. We are to become changed people who live out the reality of God.

Seeing God isn't for the purpose of being wowed.

ONE MORE EXPERIENCE WITH GOD

About a year ago I woke up early one morning and saw the strangest sight. Condensation had collected on one of my bedroom windows. Etched in the condensation were two perfectly drawn circles, joined at the center and looking exactly like wedding bands.

Staring at the design, I tried to come up with a reasonable explanation. I could not for the life of me figure out how two perfect circles could have gotten drawn into the condensation of my very-high-up bedroom window.

Later that day I went back to look at the window, but the hot afternoon sun had long since evaporated the moisture. The wedding bands were gone. For days I looked for their return, waking each morning eager to see them and ponder their existence. But when the days turned into weeks I eventually stopped looking.

Then one morning they reappeared. Only this time they were there for several mornings straight. Each morning when my eyes would open, the two etched wedding bands were the first thing I'd see.

On about the fourth morning, my heart started aching as I viewed the spectacle. An urgency suddenly pulsed through my chest. I tried to brush it off, but couldn't. It was a conviction. Not a condemning conviction. Rather, a tender one.

A tender conviction to love my husband more intentionally. And not just in the convenient ways. But in the inconvenient as well. In ways that take a little more thought ... intentionality ... and effort. Ways that are easy to let slip when the everyday urgencies seem to take precedence or seem more important.

I mentally made all kinds of promises and grand plans for a priority overhaul. And for a few days, I did great. But then life happened ... lots of life. The window circles soon disappeared and so did my resolve. I slipped back into my comfortable, getting-by pattern.

Well, at the risk of starting to sound like a Hallmark movie, the circles are back. I don't want to sound presumptuous. But the circles seem so perfectly drawn. And so perfectly timed. Do you think that maybe, just maybe, love of the most divine kind has tipped down to touch an ordinary glass window?

I do.

And I'm equally convinced that God wants to speak to and reveal Himself to you in your day-to-day life. If only you will open up your heart to the possibilities for Him to use everyday things to change you, grow you, strengthen you, and remind you of His amazing love ... you will start to see Him. You will start to hear Him. You will get to know Him more deeply. And you will want to follow Him more boldly. And what a glorious sense of possibility that is!

Part 6

IN MY CALLING

I've wanted a red coat for years. But paying full price for a coat seems excessive when I have several perfectly fine coats in my closet. So, each year I've decided to wait until coats go on clearance and then I'd treat myself.

But every year, by the time the coats went on clearance, the weather flipflopped. And who wants to spend their clothing budget on a red coat when just the thought of walking outside makes you sweat?

Then at last I happened upon a discount clothing store that was having a clearance sale. In the window was a red coat. On sale! While it was still cold outside!

I wanted to get the coat right then. However, I had a store coupon for an additional 50 percent off one item that wasn't good until a week later. That would make the coat a most fabulous deal, one that a girl could proudly wear and tell all her friends about. Yes, ma'am.

So I hung my treasure back on the rack, determined to return and get it a week later.

Two days afterward I was out and about when my husband proudly called to tell me he'd taken several of our bed comforters to the local coin laundromat. He'd gotten up that day and decided it was comforter washing day. I very much appreciated his thoughtfulness, but panic arose in my chest when he told me he'd left the comforters in the dryer and wondered if I might pick them up. I was certain they'd be gone. Rule number one with the coin laundromat: never leave stuff unsupervised.

Much to my delight, the comforters were calmly waiting for me when I arrived. While gathering them up, I saw a woman with two young children, all wearing threadbare clothing. I made small talk with the kids about what a fun time of year Christmas is; they looked away and didn't say a word. Out of the corner of my eye, I saw their mom hang her head. I wished them a Merry Christmas and scurried out.

As soon as I started to drive off, God pricked my heart. "You looked at those kids, but chose not to really see them. Go back. Help them. Help her."

But I was in a hurry. I didn't have any cash. How could I help? What would she think of me? Would I offend her by giving her a check? I didn't even know her name to write on a check.

I put the car in park, pulled out my checkbook, and suddenly I knew the exact amount I was to give her. The full price of that red coat.

I walked back into the laundromat and handed her the check. "You'll just need to write your name on this, and I promise my bank will cash it. It's not much, but I'd love for you to take it and buy your kids something fun for Christmas."

Shocked, she thanked me. As I turned to leave, she called out her name, the name God has engraved on the palm of His hand, the one He loves and hears and cares so deeply about.

Funny enough, I went into the red coat store the next day to return some pants I'd gotten. Every one of those red coats I'd wanted so much was gone. So I bought a red scarf on clearance instead and smiled, for in that moment, I knew I'd fulfilled my calling for this page of my life.

As we start this last section of the book—becoming more than a good Bible study girl in our calling—I want to make sure you know a couple of things. You do have a calling, a unique and wondrous calling from God every day of your life. Today it could be in your local laundromat; tomorrow it could be a phone conversation with a friend. Wherever it is, whatever it is, you were created to participate in God's divine activity.

My calling is as a mom, wife, speaker, writer, and friend. Your calling may look completely different. (I certainly hope you spend less time in the laundry room than I do.) But, whatever the details of your life, we have one thing in common—we were absolutely made to discover our love story with God. In the next three chapters, we'll learn what it means to live completely with God wherever He has put us, discover the power of dangerous prayers, and catch a glimpse of the breathtaking moment for which our souls were made.

Hold on, sister, the last leg of this journey will be one wild ride.

Chapter 16

FINDING GOD
IN UNLIKELY PLACES

I'll never forget the first time I attended a publishing convention, giddy with excitement and weighed down with fifteen copies of my book proposal. I was more on a mission than a college senior looking for a diamond-toting man willing to grant her a Mrs. degree.

Yes, ma'am. My shoes and I clippity-clapped all around that convention floor making appointments and praying that someone, anyone, would like the words I had all packaged up in the professional purple binders.

Because, really, nothing says "bestselling author" like a purple Office Max binder.

My last appointment of the day was with one of the biggest and most respected companies in the Christian publishing world. I couldn't believe they were even willing to talk to me. Seriously, I kept pinching myself while sitting in their appointment waiting area. It looked convincing and classy to have red pinch marks all down my arms when meeting with this publisher. Really.

The pitch went okay, but I watched as the publisher put my beloved manuscript in a tall stack with what seemed like hundreds of other people's beloved manuscripts. And then he scooted me off with some version of the famous last words, "Don't call us, we'll call you."

But all was not lost because, outside the meeting room, a famous author was doing a "meet and greet." She was BIG TIME! And while

I was excited about standing in line to meet her and get a free signed copy of her book, I was more excited about the tray of chocolate-covered strawberries awaiting on the other side. I hadn't eaten all day. Those strawberries were an oasis in the midst of a dry and weary desert of rejection.

Who needs a book contract when you can hand a starving woman a strawberry covered with the cure of all disappointment—chocolate? I barely remember meeting the author and I'm not even sure I took a copy of her book, but I will never forget the deliciousness that was bound up in that one little red berry.

It was so good, in fact, that I had to have another. But the lady holding the strawberry tray had the only-take-one-or-else look in her eye. So, I came up with the brilliant plan to just go through the line again. I mean, really, who would remember *me*?

I stood in line again, met the author again, and finally a second strawberry was mine for the taking. I reached out, my mouth watering to the point I had to suck in vast amounts of air to keep from drooling. Right as my fingers were perfectly poised to score the berry, a slap that could be heard 'round the world suddenly stunned my hand.

Everything started moving in slow motion at that point. Every eye looked my way. And the strawberry guard scolded me in very dramatic fashion:

Y-O-U–C-A-N-N-O-T–H-A-V-E–A-N-O-T-H-E-R–S-T-R-A-W-B-E-R-R-Y!

I would have paid lots of money to have the convention floor open up and swallow me whole. I would forever be known as the glutton wannabe author who tried to take two strawberries and got her hand slapped at the convention. Until, that is, everyone forgot about it two seconds later. But me and my clippity-clap shoes have never forgotten that day.

Many years later, having weathered many, many rejection letters, I finally made it back to that same convention. This time as an author of that very publisher. And instead of toting purple bound book proposals, I was in my hotel room preparing to go to the convention floor for my own book signing.

Again, I was nervous. And again, I was decorating my arms with red pinch marks when there was a knock at the door. I opened it and couldn't help but double over in laughter at what the bellman handed me.

Me and my clippity-clap shoes thanked him, closed the door, and twirled about that hotel room holding the biggest tray of chocolate-covered strawberries you've ever seen!

SEEING THE GOOD IN HARD THINGS

Life does have a way of eventually coming around. Sometimes it's in the way we hope, and other times it's in completely surprising ways. The apostle Paul's words have comforted me and helped me press on when I honestly felt too weak to face another day:

> In the same way, the Spirit helps us in our weakness. We do not know what we ought to pray for, but the Spirit himself intercedes for us with groans that words cannot express. And he who searches our hearts knows the mind of the Spirit, because the Spirit intercedes for the saints in accordance with God's will. And we know that in all things God works for the good of those who love him, who have been called according to his purpose. (Romans 8:26–28)

Notice a couple things about this passage. It doesn't say that God works all things in a way that makes us happy. Nor does it say that God does things in the timing we desire.

Seeing the good come from hard things takes time. But it can be time well spent if it leads us to realize that it is more important to follow God than to follow what *we* think is the best path for our life.

If I could have written the script for my life, I would have written a much shorter route to getting published. I definitely would have left out all the rejection letters and hand slapping. But I now realize the purpose for all of that. It humbled me and taught me the beauty of trusting God to direct my life (James 4:10).

Seeing the good come from hard things takes time.

Not getting those opportunities sooner were not God's way of *keeping me from* my calling; they were His way of *preparing me for* it. This humbling process wound up being thrilling. I found God in deep ways during those lonely days of writing book proposals that were never published and articles that only my friends enjoyed. But God was faithful, and although my ministry was very small-scale for years, it was still fruitful.

God used that preparation time to teach me how to be passionate about following only His plans. Becoming more than a good Bible study girl means waiting for God's timing, waiting for the good He is working in us. And when we're ready to move forward, becoming a good Bible study girl means remembering to help those coming along just behind us. This ensures that our calling is not just about us.

REMEMBERING THOSE JUST BEHIND ME

I recently attended a Chick-fil-A convention with my husband, Art, who owns one of the restaurants in this popular chain. Chick-fil-A conventions are more like revivals than business meetings. This year was no exception, as many of the speakers challenged us to pursue God like never before.

After one of the sessions I beelined it to the bathroom like any woman would who was filled with too much coffee, water, and diet soda. A long line had already formed, and I had to wait my turn until a stall opened up. When I finally reached my destination, I realized the woman before me had left her conference notebook behind.

I didn't see who had just exited that particular stall so I looked around the bathroom for someone who was empty-handed. Unsuccessful at finding the owner in the bathroom, I flipped open the binder to see if a name was written inside, and the first handwriting I saw was the words "ministry to women." At the risk of being totally nosy, I kept reading. Basically what the owner of the notebook had written was that this would be the year she would finally get intentional about pursuing the ministry to women God had placed on her heart.

As I read those words, I felt Jesus' invitation, "Follow Me," and didn't hesitate to say yes. You see, in my journey to live completely with God every day, I have learned the treasure of expectation. I ask God to help me live in expectation of experiencing Him; therefore, I do. It's not that I go around getting involved in every situation around me. But I do ask God to make me wise and aware of which opportunities are mine. This day, I knew exactly how to follow Jesus completely in this situation.

As I exited the bathroom, I ran into Mark, a dear friend of ours who works at the Chick-fil-A corporate office. He was headed in the direction of the conference information desk, and so I asked him if he would put the notebook in "lost and found" for me. I paused before I handed him the book and quickly told him what I'd seen written inside.

"I think I'm supposed to write a note inside her book," I said.

"Go ahead," he said. "I'll wait."

At the risk of having this woman think I was crazy, I pulled out my pen and simply wrote off to the side, "I might be able to help you with this. Call me, if you'd like. Lysa TerKeurst with Proverbs 31 Ministries." I added my cell phone number and handed the book to Mark.

Days went by, the conference ended, and I never heard from anyone. Almost a week later, I'd forgotten about the whole thing. And then the call came.

From the start of my conversation with Tracey, I could tell that God Himself had arranged this divine encounter. To make a long story short, my simple note was the confirmation from God for which she'd been fervently praying. Tracey and I were both blown away. Later, she sent me this note expressing her thoughts:

Lysa,

I was completely freaked out when I saw your note in my book! It was like God had written me a personal note to tell me that He loves me and that He knows the desires of my heart and that no one else is going to make this happen but Him. My heart was racing, my hands started to shake, and I could not hear anything else that was going on in the room! I honestly just stared at it in disbelief for quite a while. What are the chances that out of 1,500 women at that conference and hundreds of bathroom stalls that I would leave my book in one that you would stumble upon? Then, on top of that, what are the chances that you would open to the very page that I had written my vision on and read it?

It was truly a supernatural arrangement. It confirmed to me that God has not only placed this desire in my heart, but He will go to great lengths to see it fulfilled! There is no stopping me now! I have been through several months of great heaviness and now I know what it was all about. Something GREAT is right around the corner. Just within the past week, after speaking with you, God has begun to open up doors like you would not believe. (Well, I guess you would!) Thank you for your obedience in writing the note and for being such an inspiration!

Tracey

My encounter with Tracey was yet another reminder that the more we follow Jesus, the more we fall in love with Him, want to obey Him, experience life with Him, and become a beacon of light to others through Him.

Do you feel a tug at your heart to live completely with God, but are still uncertain about pursuing it? Why not ask God to reveal Himself to you in the coming days and confirm exactly what He has for you? The adventure that follows just might blow you away.

Will it be inconvenient? Maybe.

Will it cost you in ways that stretch you? Sometimes.

Does it force you to live life with a less self-centered outlook? Yes.

Does living to follow Jesus at every turn bring joy that you can't get any other way? Absolutely.

It is the very thing your soul was created to do. It is the most daily way to discover your purpose in life.

Recently, I read a blog entry that deeply touched me. The author is Lisa Spence, a woman who is learning to find her purpose by daily waiting, watching, and wanting nothing more than Christ alone.

Lisa desires to be in ministry. She's sought God and asked Him to make His plans clear to her. Because she loves to teach God's Word and feels God has gifted her to do this, she wondered if He might have her become a speaker or teacher. She waited for the phone call of opportunity to ring. It did not.

Lisa also loves to write and found out that a major Christian publisher was accepting unsolicited manuscripts for women's Bible studies. She wrote a proposal, furiously editing and frantically rewriting, and finally sent it off. Maybe this was her chance to step into ministry! It wasn't.

The Lord is indeed faithful and through both of these experiences, He taught Lisa the value of the common life. In her blog, she shared her tender revelations:

> It became my privilege to serve Him whether He called me to the big or the little. To exalt Him as my greatest Treasure in the midst of the mundane, in car line, in laundry, in blogging, and even in occasionally cleaning house.

A month or so ago, I was part of a conversation where someone described a fellow professional with great excitement, speaking of her excellence and great potential in her profession.

For the first time ever, I feared I had made a mistake. My heart froze as I wondered if I was supposed to be something, do something. I know it sounds foolish, but I longed for someone to speak of me and my potential in such glowing terms.

As I felt that familiar stab of fear and insecurity over my place in this world, I see I am learning the same lesson once again—I am in a place that is only from the Lord.

Here, choosing contentment when the world tells me to strive for accomplishment. Only He could bring me to this. Only He can show me the great joy of doing everything—everything and anything!—for His glory. Only He is worth more than any joy of this world, even writing Bible studies or speaking at women's events! Only He is worthy and only He is worth laying it all down, all of it.

What do you think you need? What do you think you want? What do I? Let's lay it down and find ourselves where we never dreamed we'd be: counting it all as rubbish compared to the surpassing glory of knowing Christ! He is the only Treasure worth pursuing![16]

Too many people think that finding the reason God placed us here on earth will come in one lump assignment with a big title and complete job description. I believe that discovering our purpose will unfold slowly, like a seed planted deep in the ground.

Each day, a seed embraces the task placed before it. Today it might have to embrace the dark soil it has been pushed into. Tomorrow, it might be not resisting the water that makes it literally disintegrate and fall apart. And then in a week or two, a green shoot pushes up and out of the deep, dark, messy place. Eventually, the seed sprouts and reveals exactly what it was always meant to be. The seed's potential is unlocked and its purpose is revealed through embracing each and every circumstance God brought its way. Isn't it glorious how nature doesn't resist God? Sadly, too many of God's people cannot say the same.

So, just for today I will live this way. Just for today, I am making the choice to not settle. Just for today, I will not let the subtle influences of pride and thinking I know what is best for me overshadow my desire for more of God in my life. Today, I will believe with absolute certainty. Today, I will obey with complete surrender. Today, I will seek with complete abandon. For doing this is fulfilling the purpose for which I was created ... not to bring myself glory by some great accomplishment but to bring God glory by making Him my greatest heart's desire.

O God, let me make that choice today. Even if it is just for a day—how I long for it to be more—but even if it is just for today, may it be completely so. For one day completely with You is truly, truly better than a thousand elsewhere.

Isn't it glorious how nature doesn't resist God?
Sadly, too many of God's people cannot say the same.

Why do I often want to settle for less than what God has for me? What if I truly lived today completely obedient to God's Word and in tune with His voice? What if before every choice I make today, I held up my options to the Lord and chose obedience over convenience and righteousness over my rights.

God has never asked me to do great things for Him. All He has ever required of me is to allow His greatness to enter me, change me from within, and be revealed through me. Not to do *for* Him, but rather to simply *be with* Him. And when this earthly adventure is done and I meet God face-to-face maybe, just maybe, we'll enjoy a big platter of chocolate-covered strawberries together.

Chapter 17

PRAYING THE DANGEROUS PRAYERS

Each summer my family and I spend a week at a family camp in the Adirondack Mountains. I love this place. My husband loves this place. And though our kids range from elementary school to college, they all love this place. Combine spectacular surroundings with fun family time and you've got quite a vacation.

But isn't it funny that even when everything seems perfect, little things … little stupid things … can chip away at your heart's peace? This can especially happen when we fall into the trap of making the focus of our prayers what we want from God rather than God Himself.

A few years ago Art and I were scheduled to speak at this camp on the theme "Giving Your Family a Spiritual Vision." I might as well have had a red target on my forehead that read "Bring it on, Satan."

The attack started first thing that morning with a shower timing situation. Four teenagers, one nine-year-old princess, and a hubby who likes to be clean all sharing one small bathroom in one small cabin. A bonding opportunity on good days, but not so much today.

I was the last in the shower. And I had the most to do to get ready. *Hola, la familia? Who has to speak today, and who just simply needs to saunter into teen chapel?*

Ahem.

When I finally got all 38,472 hairs on my head washed, dried, straightened, and sprayed, I started clippity-clapping my little speaker shoes through camp.

That's about the point a sudden rain shower decided to mock all my preparation efforts. My Bible proved to be a handy shelf to at least block my bangs. And, really, the protection of Southern-style bangs is of the utmost importance.

I finally made it into the auditorium with only half my head looking like a wadded-up frizzball. And then I realized with all the spraying and straightening and Bible-bangs-holding, I had forgotten my notes ALLLLL the way back in the cabin.

Have mercy.

You've got to be kidding me.

At this point I wasn't feeling any kind of spiritual vision much less wanting to speak about it for the next hour — an hour in which I would be required to stand before fellow humans looking strangely like a drowned rat with some serious frizz on her 'fro of a hairdo.

Have you ever wished Scotty could beam you up? I would have been delighted to be reduced into a million space particles if it meant I'd be able to pop back to the cabin to retrieve my notes without having to go back out in the rain. But since Scotty only beams people up in episodes where people trek through stars and not a rain-soaked camp, I started clippity-clapping back across camp.

I was having an honest talk with the Lord about His timing of rain showers. Okay, I was pouting and whining. "Don't you see me, Lord? Why the rain right now?"

All of a sudden, a friend came out of nowhere with an open umbrella and simply said, "Lysa, you need this." I thanked her, took the umbrella, and continued on ... dryly. I peaked up and over the edge of the umbrella at the sky.

I smiled.

God had once again provided for me. But only after I'd gotten wet, frustrated, and come face-to-face with something pretty ugly in my heart.

Why was I questioning whether or not God cared about me? So a little rain fell in my life that day. So the events leading up to my talk weren't exactly great. So my hair was frizzy and my notes a tad wet and smeared. Why couldn't I just take it all in stride and negate Satan's nagging voice right from the get-go?

I realized that most times it's not the big things along my spiritual journey that tempt me to get off track. It's a culmination of small daily aggravations I know God could fix but doesn't.

But what if instead of seeing these aggravations as inconveniences, I saw them as reminders to draw near to God? Doesn't the Bible say, "Draw near to God and He will draw near to you" (James 4:8)? My rain-soaked, frizzy-haired, clippity-clap-shoes-wearing, notes-retrieving self determined that this unplanned trek had done me a lot of good.

What if instead of seeing aggravations as inconveniences, I saw them as reminders to draw near to God?

At dusk that same day, I was sitting on my bed talking to God while gazing out the window at a most glorious sunset. Suddenly I felt much like I did the first time that my stepdad and I had a heart-to-heart adult conversation after I had kids of my own—though I still held a deep respect for him as my parent figure, I had somehow graduated to the privilege of also being his friend.

This was the way I was feeling with God that night. As if I were just having a casual conversation with both my heavenly Father *and* my friend. I'll never be able to explain how it is possible for God to be both at the same time.

Is this thought slightly irreverent? No, but it is shocking. God was taking time to speak to me. Tender suggestions were flooding my mind, things I would have never thought of on my own. I knew they were from the Lord.

Bits and pieces of Scripture were woven throughout, and it made me smile. It confirmed that this was, in fact, God speaking. And it made our conversation comfortable and familiar. Just like a friend who has certain ways of saying things. As they talk, you can almost finish some of their sentences because you know exactly where they're headed in the conversation.

This wasn't an official prayer time with God. I didn't have my head bowed, my hands folded, or my eyes closed. And I wasn't seeking answers from the Lord. As a matter of fact, for the first time in a long while, I wasn't asking God for anything at all. I was just sitting in His presence, simply being with Him.

In his book *Personal God,* Tim Stafford writes, "Getting answers to your prayers is not enough. A machine does that at your request. Put a dollar in a vending machine, and you will get something out. Only a friend, though, will talk to you about what troubles you or offer advice as you ponder your life direction."[17]

In this casual but very holy time, I told God how badly I felt that something as trivial as a rain shower and a bad hairdo could make me feel off-kilter. I almost expected God to sweetly respond about how many hairs I had on my head and how He loves them all, no matter if they are frizzy or straight.

Instead, I suddenly came to understand a slight flaw in my prayer life. As I thought about the way I prayed, I realized how often my prayers seemed to center around ways I wanted God to bless me:

> *God, bless my kids and keep them safe.*
> *God, bless me and my family with good health and strong, capable bodies.*
> *God, bless my ministry and help us to effectively reach people for You.*
> *God, bless my home that it might always be an oasis for those who live there and those who visit.*

God, bless my husband's business.
God, bless my kid's efforts at school.
God, bless this food that You so richly provide.
God, bless our day today.
God, bless me as I prepare to speak in Your name and keep
the rain from messing with my hair and my notes.

Now, none of these are bad prayers, if there even is such a thing as a bad prayer. They are honest prayers, heartfelt prayers, common prayers, the prayers of many women who are rising to the daunting task of caring for their families. Okay, all but that last prayer — that one was just my issue.

But they are slightly flawed prayers because they set my expectations of God to be what I want without taking into consideration the possibility of God's bigger plan. I make God into One who stunts my growth with convenience and comfort rather than One who grows me into a woman of character, perseverance, and maturity.

We merely want to scratch the surface of the promise Jesus offers when He says, "Ask and it will be given to you; seek and you will find; knock and the door will be opened to you. For everyone who asks receives; he who seeks finds; and to him who knocks, the door will be opened" (Luke 11:9 – 10). Yes, we want the promises, but we don't want to get any dirt under our fingernails in the process. We want comfortable circumstances, but we resist any transformational changes that might be necessary. Oh, how we want the gifts promised here, but I wonder if the real treasure is to get to the place where we want the Giver most of all.

We want the promises, but we don't want to get
any dirt under our fingernails in the process.

Nancy Guthrie once wrote an article entitled, "Prayers That Move the Heart of God." In this fascinating piece she says,

> There's so much to want—healed bodies, restored relationships, changed circumstances. But asking, seeking, and knocking aren't secret formulas for getting what we want *from* God; they're ways to get more *of* God. As I listen to God speak to me through his Word, he gives me more of himself in fuller, newer ways. Then, if healing doesn't come, if the relationship remains broken, or if the pressures increase, I have the opportunity to discover for myself he is enough. His presence is enough. His purpose is enough.[18]

Nancy goes on to share that by changing her prayers to be more about getting to know God rather than getting what she wants from Him, she is beginning to experience Him in deeper ways than ever before.

Author John Piper echoes this theme: "When humans forsake their Maker and love other things more, they become like the things they love—small, insignificant, weightless, inconsequential, and God diminishing."[19]

How I long to never diminish God by loving lesser things. Rather, I want to make much of God by diminishing lesser things. May I make less of me, less of this world, less of the temporary ... so that I may be a vessel more full of God, more full of eternal perspectives, more full of His everlasting! Is this your desire too? Maybe it's time we pray more dangerous prayers.

DANGEROUS PRAYERS

The most logical question to ask in light of everything else in this chapter might be, "So then, how should we pray?" But instead of asking *how*, we should be asking *why*: Why do we pray? To get things, or to get God?

I still present my requests to God, but I try to resist making them the focus of my prayers. Instead, I'm learning to focus on three plain-and-simple things: aligning my heart with God's heart; escaping from my own selfish perspectives of life; and listening, really listening, to God.

Instead of filling up my prayer time with *my* words, I want to spend more time hearing whatever *He* might have to say. Power enters our prayers not by sounding powerful, but by listening for even the slightest whisper from the One who is all-powerful. That was the beautiful thing about my time with the Lord that evening at camp, watching that amazing sunset.

Power enters our prayers not by sounding powerful,
but by listening for even the slightest whisper
from the One who is all-powerful.

After sitting with Him for a long while, listenening to the gentle convictions coursing through my heart that I knew were from Him, I finally spoke out loud: "Forgive me for always praying, *God, bless me.* Give me the courage to sometimes pray, *God, inconvenience me ... so that I might constantly be reminded to draw near to You. Interrupt me, Lord. Shake things up in me, Lord. Reveal what's in me that's not of You, Lord. O Lord, more than anything, I want more of You.*"

At that moment, I could hear my friend Suzy yelling from outside our cabin, "Lysa, come look." I assumed she wanted me to see the sunset. But when I got outside and turned in the direction she was pointing, it was not the sunset but a glorious rainbow stretching across our cabin. It made my breath catch in my throat.

The panoramic view of the sky that night was unlike any I've ever seen. On one side of the mountain range, the clouds swirled and mixed with the sun's setting rays, and on the other side beamed a magnificent arch of color and promise. I grabbed my heart as I felt God's creation exclaim, "The Lord is not just near ... He is delighting, dancing, speaking, wooing, and painting in your midst."

That's the beauty of praying these dangerous prayers, inviting the divine presence into otherwise mundane moments. They are dangerous prayers not because they bring danger into our lives. They are dangerous because they will not leave us unchanged—and most of us consider change downright frightening. For this season of my life, my dangerous prayers are:

> *God, inconvenience me ... so that I might constantly be reminded to draw near to You.*
> *Interrupt me, Lord.*
> *Shake things up in me, Lord.*
> *Reveal what's in me that's not of You, Lord.*
> *And, Lord, more than anything, I want more of You.*

But please don't use these as a formula or checklist. Come up with your own dangerous prayers to weave into your everyday conversations with God. Spend some time, as I did, basking in God's creation, listening to Him.

You may hear nothing at first. The silence may be deafening, frustrating, slightly disappointing. But don't stop sitting with God. At some point, when God is the deepest desire of your heart, you will hear Him.

Just as God promised Jeremiah that He would bring His people back from exile, He will be faithful to draw our heart out of the chaos it's grown accustomed to into the sweet stillness of His presence. "'Then you will call upon me and come and pray to me, and I will listen to you. You will seek me and find me when you seek me with all your heart. I will be found by you,' declares the LORD, 'and will bring you back from captivity'" (Jeremiah 29:12–14).

Whether our captivity is our own self-centeredness, fear of change, doubts about whether or not God really speaks to people, or uncertainty that we'd want to hear what He might have to say to us—we can be free. Free to hear from Him. Free to experience life with Him. And, best of all, free to become more and more like Him.

As I think back to that day full of rain showers, smeared notes, and frizzy hair, I see things so much differently. Had I known the gift that day would bring, I wouldn't have cared so much about the tiny aggravations. Seeing that rainbow stretch across the sky was worth every drop of rain that inconvenienced me.

My hope now is to remember the glorious outcome of that day. So that when the rains come in the future, as they most certainly will, I'll be reminded to pray more dangerously and to live more expectantly of experiencing the God who resides in our midst.

Chapter 18

FOREVER

It was one of the most beautiful marriage ceremonies I'd ever attended. Notice I didn't say weddings. I've been to elaborate weddings before where the emphasis was placed on peripheral details: lavish floral displays, banquet tables full of rich foods, intricately designed cakes, exquisite gowns.

This one was different. The focal point was the couple.

The music crescendo signaled us to all stand as the back doors of the church opened. The father of the bride delicately took his daughter's arm and led her down the aisle toward her groom. She was beaming. The groom was awestruck. The father bit his bottom lip to stop it from quivering as tears slipped down his cheeks.

I wondered which memories flashed across the screen of his mind in this tender moment, as the last threads of his daughter's childhood were slowly being snipped from his heart. What memories tugged at his emotions as he took this last walk with his little girl? Was he remembering her as a baby being placed in his arms for the first time? Or did he see a toddler donning a pink tutu, twirling about the kitchen? Or the day he took her to kindergarten, looking so grown-up with her backpack and lunchbox? Maybe it was the emotional days of adolescence where he comforted her first broken heart. Or the day she first brought this young man home with a gleam in her eye so telling he knew she'd soon be a bride.

As they reached the end of the red-carpeted aisle, the pastor announced the father had a special presentation he wanted to make before releasing his daughter in marriage. The father then walked over to a small pillow being carried by one of the ring bearers and untied a simple gold ring. Looking straight into the groom's misty eyes, the father held up the ring.

"When my daughter was young, I gave her this ring as she promised to stay pure for her husband. It is with great honor that I present this ring to you as a symbol of her commitment to you before she even knew you." Then, extending his hand to the groom, he gave him the ring as he let go of his daughter's hand.

Not a dry eye could be found in the church that day.[20]

A BRIDE AGAIN

I have thought about the beauty of what was symbolized in that ceremony many times. I long for this same scenario for each of my children.

But I also long for it for myself. Sounds strange coming from a woman like me, doesn't it? Not only am I already married but, as you know from my life story, I had not saved myself for my wedding day.

My longing is no longer one of regret. Though I wish I'd protected my purity, I've made peace with the fact that I can't go back and change things. I can, however, move forward. God has forgiven me, healed me, and restored my marriage in amazing ways. God is a God of redemption and for that I am very thankful.

No, my longing isn't centered in my past at all. My longing is now one of anticipation. Because the reality is, I will be a bride again. And the next time I want to walk that aisle with a gift of purity for my heavenly Groom. It will be my heart. Though it will be an imperfect gift, I want God to announce to Jesus that my journey through life helped me grow a heart totally and purely devoted to Him.

Here is what the last book of the Bible says about the triumphant day when we will be reunited with Christ: "Then I heard what sounded like a great multitude, like the roar of rushing waters and like loud peals of thunder, shouting: 'Hallelujah! For our Lord God Almighty reigns. Let us rejoice and be glad and give him glory! For the wedding of the Lamb has come, and his bride has made herself ready'" (Revelation 19:6–7).

We, the church, are that bride. And Jesus is the bridegroom. Probably one of the most quoted verses about marriage in the Bible is Ephesians 5:31, itself a quote of Genesis 2:24: "For this reason a man will leave his father and mother and be united to his wife, and the two will become one flesh." Now read the very next verse—Ephesians 5:32, "This is a profound mystery—but I am talking about Christ and the church."

Maybe this is why great love stories stir something in us. We were made for the greatest love story of them all. We were made to fall in love with Jesus.

We were made for the greatest love story of them all.

But we can't fall in love with Jesus while holding Him at a distance. We can't fall in love just by reading factual details about Him. We will only fall in love when we draw close, deepen our understanding of Him, and seek to do life with Him.

Consider the words of Isaiah: "Thus says the LORD, 'Heaven is My throne and the earth is My footstool. Where then is a house you could build for Me? And where is a place that I may rest? For My hand made all these things, thus all these things came into being,' declares the LORD. 'But to this one I will look, to him who is humble and contrite of spirit, and who trembles at My word'" (Isaiah 66:1–2 NASB).

My soul jumps at these questions, "Where is the house you could build for me? And where is a place that I may rest?" He is the God of the universe—so big and so mighty and so capable. Yet He asks almost a vulnerable question to a completely unworthy human, "May I abide with you today?" If the president of the United States called me today to inquire, "May I come and stay for a while? I'd like to sit and rest with your family today," I would be left utterly speechless. How much more so that the God of the universe actually desires to be with each of us today.

Unimaginable. Uncontainable. Unfathomable. Yet completely true.

ABANDON

I long to live a life pleasing to Jesus. Not a plastic Christian life full of religious checklists and pretense. No, that would be hypocritical at best and deadening at worst.

I want to live completely with Jesus. Captured by His love. Enthralled with His teachings. Living proof of His truth.

Others who have gone before me have desired this as well. I am fascinated by the imperfect heroes of faith who, despite their short-comings, pleased God. But don't you find the sins of those men and women a little unsettling at times? Part of me wants them to be perfect, so I can set a standard in my life. Like a child gingerly making her way through the sand by placing her feet exactly in her mother's footprints, I want to find the hallmarks of their journeys and follow in step.

But God never called me to follow them. Or to make my journey like theirs. It wasn't their perfect actions that carved a path to God's heart. It was something else. Something less defined, that can't be outlined and dissected. Something that was occasionally messy and offensive. But something that was so precious it caused God to pause.

"Abandon."

Interesting word choice, don't you think? It means "to leave com-pletely, to forsake." When misplaced, this word can have horrible implications. I know. It is the exact thing my earthly father did to me and my family. However, when properly placed, it plays a crucial role in every love story.

Wrapped in most wedding vows, the pastor will usually challenge the couple to repeat some version of this statement, "Will you have this man to be your husband, to live together in the covenant of marriage? Will you love him, comfort him, honor and keep him, in sickness and in health, and, *forsaking all others*, be faithful to him as long as you both shall live?"

This forsaking of all others is vital to a successful marriage. Abandoning the casual to gain the permanent. Leaving behind anything that would hinder the commitment.

In the best sense of the word, I will abandon.

That's what I believe causes God to pause. It's the word used to describe a child leaping from the edge of the bed, completely confident that her daddy will catch her. It's the same thing that fueled David's courageous run at Goliath with nothing but a sling and five smooth stones. It fueled Joshua. And Moses. And Noah. And Paul.

Everything I have. Everything I own. Everything I hope for. Everything I fear. Everything I love. Everything I dream. It's all Yours, Jesus. I trust You in complete and utter abandon.

Abandon. It's the one thing that made the rich young ruler sadly walk away in the story told in Luke 18. He had asked Jesus how to inherit eternal life. A life of peace, assurance, joy despite circumstances, and eternal security. "How do I get this?" he wondered. "I follow the rules. I'm a good person."

Jesus was quick to reply, "You still lack one thing." Release. Let go of. Stop depending on. Cease striving for. Abandon. "Sell everything you have and follow me."

The rich young ruler stood uncertain on the edge of everything, with the arms of all certainty waiting to catch him. And he just couldn't jump. He climbed off the bed. And lived his life entangled in lesser things. Instead of forsaking the trappings of this world, he chose to forsake the love his soul was made for.

He was not captured by, enthralled with, or living proof of the reality of Jesus.

God, let this not be the tragedy of our lives.

Give me the courage to make my own path straight to Your heart. That though it will not be perfect, I pray it is marked with that which makes You pause—complete abandon to my will but utterly surrendered to Yours.

UTTERLY SURRENDERED TO GOD'S PLANS

I was talking with a friend the other day when she asked me the most interesting question: "What are your plans for the next five years?" I used to have a well-thought-out answer. I might even have had an entire organized goal sheet full of purpose statements, Scripture verses, and time lines.

Now, lest you become impressed, don't be. It would not be neatly typed on the computer, with words boldfaced and highlighted and fancy. No, it would be scratched on the back of a napkin and stuffed in the bottom of my purse. It would most certainly be full of crumbs and maybe even a chewed piece of gum. I'm highly organized like that.

I would take great comfort in knowing where I was headed, and having it all written down would give me a greater chance of getting there. As identified on my official napkin document. These weren't willy-nilly goals. I had prayed through them and looked for confirmations. These were good plans, surrendered-to-the-Lord plans, plans I hoped He would bless.

But that's not where I am today. So, perhaps to my friend's surprise, I just quietly replied, "I have no idea."

I went on to explain that I do have things I'd like to accomplish, but I just can't get all determined by writing them down and then setting about to check them off my list. I used to live that way. But then God shook things up a bit and helped me understand the truth of

Proverbs 19:21, which says, "Many are the plans in a man's heart, but it is the LORD's purpose that prevails."

God promises many times in the Bible that He has a plan for our lives. Since our lives are lived moment by moment, that must mean that He has a purpose for each of our minutes, each of our hours, each of our days. When I stopped to think about this, I realized my plans for my future had become so consuming that I had stopped considering God's purpose for right now. I stopped looking for God in this moment. I stopped lingering with Him and considering His activity right in front of me. I stopped remaining and abiding closely with Him.

I started viewing this moment as something I just had to get through so I could move on to better things in the future, my great plans. I wrongly discerned that only meeting my future goals would bring satisfaction, significance, and self-worth.

I'm not saying that making plans, setting goals, and seeking accomplishments are bad things. I think having a set of goals is a good thing for many people. But when having a goal takes your focus off God and His daily intentions for you, it can cause trouble.

Being driven by my plans can shift the focus of my heart from following God and being open to His unfolding invitations to following only that which leads me closer to my desires. For me, I started falling into a trap of making plans each day around what I wanted to see happen. Anything that wasn't a part of my plan became a distraction and an unwelcome irritation.

When having a goal takes your focus off God and His daily intentions for you, it can cause trouble.

Proverbs 29:18 (KJV) says, "Where there is no vision, the people perish." People have often taught that verse as direction from God that we should come up with a clearly defined vision and follow through with making it happen. Henry Blackaby says, "Proverbs 29:18, although widely used, is also widely misapplied.... A more accurate translation of the Hebrew is 'Where there is no revelation, people cast off restraint' (NIV). There is a significant difference between *revelation* and *vision*. Vision is something people produce; revelation is something people receive. Leaders can dream up a vision, but they cannot discover God's will. God must reveal it."[21]

Becoming more than a good Bible study girl means that we desire God's revelations in our life more than we desire our own carefully constructed plans. So easy to say, so hard to actually live out.

After all, I am no expert. I'm a simple woman who has learned the beauty of having but one simple vision for her life ...

It will be the most beautiful marriage ceremony ever held. This wedding will be unlike any other. The details will pale in comparison to the main attraction—Jesus and His bride. The heavenly choir will crescendo, signaling all the heavenly hosts to stand as the bride approaches the One who holds the answer to every longing of her heart.

Though the bride walks toward her Groom alone, the voice of her heavenly Father rushes through her heart with tender reminders. Memories start to flash across the screen of her mind with each divine whisper. She suddenly remembers so much. As the last threads of her earthly humanity are snipped away, things become crystal-clear in light of eternity. All things are made right in that moment. Questions she once thought she'd have to ask dissipate and fade. No more *why* questions. No more injustices. No more regrets. Just a peaceful assurance that whatever got her to this moment was worth it all.

And then she reaches her Groom. He has all of eternity prepared for her. The sight of it is so grand she can hardly process it. And she wonders why she ever felt tempted by the hollow things of the world. How could they have ever captured her attention compared with the glorious scene before her? How could she ever have felt content just being a Bible study girl, reading about her Groom but never really getting to know Him? Oh, how this moment is worth every effort she put forth to seek more with Him. What a journey it has been to arrive at this day.

In light of all He is giving her, she blushes at the simplicity of her gift for Him. Herself. That's it. But the Father has assured her that's all the Groom ever wanted. And within herself beats a heart that has finally learned the secret to all joy, all fulfillment, all significance, all assurance, all hope, and all security. Forsaking all else that ever grabbed for her attention, she whispers, "I am Yours, fully and completely. Forever."

NOTES

1. http://blog.christianitytoday.com/outofur/archives/2007/10/willow_creek_ re.html.
2. http://dictionary.reference.com/browse/glorious.
3. Biblegateway.com is a website that allows you to do a "keyword search": type in a word and it will bring up all the references to that word in the Bible. You can also use the "passage lookup" feature to see a certain verse in any number of Bible translations (e.g., NIV, The Message, King James Version, etc.).
4. Robert S. McGee, *The Search for Significance*, second edition (Houston: Rapha Publishing, 1990), 64–65.
5. Melanie Chitwood, "Love Covers," Proverbs 31 Ministries *Encouragement for Today* online devotion, Tuesday April 29, 2008: http://proverbs31devotions.blogspot.com/2008/04/love-covers.html. Used with permission. Melanie is also the author of the book *What a Husband Needs from His Wife*.
6. To read the specific post that includes this quote, go to: http://ebeth.typepad.com/reallearning/2008/08/eating-our-own.html. You can also visit Elizabeth's website: www.elizabethfoss.com.
7. http://www.anapsid.org/cnd/gender/tendfend.html.
8. www.LysaTerKeurst.com.
9. http://dictionary.reference.com/browse/hinder.
10. http://dictionary.reference.com/browse/entangle.
11. http://www.guttmacher.org/media/presskits/2005/06/28/abortionoverview.html.
12. http://dictionary.reference.com/browse/seek.
13. Francis Frangipane, *Holiness, Truth, and the Presence of God* (Cedar Rapids, Iowa: Arrow Publications, 1986), 77.
14. Used by permission of Whitney Capps, speaker, writer, and team member of Proverbs 31 Ministries: http://proverbs31.gospelcom.net/speakingministry/speakerteam/WhitneyCapps.php.

15. Henry Blackaby and Claude King, *Experiencing God* (Nashville: Broadman and Holman, 1994).

16. Lisa Spence blog post "Only Him" found at this link: http://lisa-writes. blogspot.com/2008/08/only-him.html.

17. Tim Stafford, *Personal God* (Grand Rapids, Mich.: Zondervan, 2007), 51.

18. Nancy Guthrie, "Prayers That Move the Heart of God," *Today's Christian Woman* 28, no. 2 (March/April 2006), 22.

19. John Piper, *Pierced by the Word* (Colorado Springs: Multnomah, 2003), 26.

20. Special thanks to Mr. and Mrs. Cozine for the beautiful example your wedding was to so many.

21. Henry and Richard Blackaby, *Spiritual Leadership* (Nashville: Broadman and Holman, 2001), 69.

ABOUT LYSA TERKEURST

Lysa TerKeurst is a wife to Art and mom to five priority blessings named Jackson, Mark, Hope, Ashley, and Brooke. She has been featured on *Focus on the Family*, *Good Morning America*, the *Oprah Winfrey Show*, and in *O Magazine*. Her greatest passion is inspiring women to say yes to God and take part in the awesome adventure He has designed every soul to live. But she always chuckles when people call her the Proverbs 31 woman. While she is the cofounder of Proverbs 31 Ministries, to those who know her best she is simply a car-pooling mom who loves her family, loves Jesus passionately, and struggles like the rest of us with laundry, junk drawers, and cellulite.

WEBSITE: If you enjoyed this book by Lysa, check out her website at: *www.LysaTerKeurst.com*.

BLOG: Dialog with Lysa through her daily blog, see pictures of her family, and follow her speaking schedule. She'd love to meet you at an event in your area!

BOOKING LYSA TO SPEAK: If you are interested in booking Lysa for a speaking engagement, contact Holly Good:

holly@proverbs31.org.

ABOUT PROVERBS 31 MINISTRIES

If you were inspired by *Becoming More Than a Good Bible Study Girl* and yearn to deepen your own personal relationship with Jesus Christ, I encourage you to connect with Proverbs 31 Ministries. Proverbs 31 Ministries exists to be a trusted friend who will take you by the hand and walk by your side, leading you one step closer to the heart of God through:

- *Encouragement for Today*, free online daily devotions
- The *P31 Woman* monthly magazine
- Daily radio program
- Books and resources
- Dynamic speakers with life-changing messages
- Online communities
- Gather and Grow groups

To learn more about Proverbs 31 Ministries or to inquire about having Lysa TerKeurst speak at your event, contact:

Holly Good (*holly@proverbs31.org*),
or visit *www.proverbs31.org*.

Proverbs 31 Ministries
616-G Matthews-Mint Hill Road
Matthews, NC 28105
www.proverbs31.org

Becoming More Than a Good Bible Study Girl DVD Curriculum

Lysa TerKeurst, President of Proverbs 31 Ministries

"I really want to know God, personally and intimately."

Those words of speaker, award-winning author, and popular blogger Lysa TerKeurst mirror the feelings of countless women. They're tired of just going through the motions of being a Christian: Go to church. Pray. Be nice. That spiritual to-do list just doesn't cut it. But what does? How can ordinary, busy moms, wives, and workers step out of the drudgery of religious duty to experience a living, moment-by-moment, deeply intimate relationship with God?

In six small group DVD sessions designed for use with the accompanying participant's guide, Lysa shows women how they can transform their walk with God from lackluster theory to vibrant reality. The *Becoming More Than a Bible Study Girl* DVD curriculum guides participants on an incredible, tremendously rewarding journey on which they will discover how to:

- Build personal, two-way conversations with God
- Study the Bible and experience life-change for themselves
- Cultivate greater authenticity and depth in their relationships
- Make disappointments work for them, not against them
- Find incredible joy as they live out their faith in everyday circumstances

DVD: 978-0-310-32206-1   Participant's Guide: 978-0-310-32208-5

Pick up a copy today at your favorite bookstore!

Share Your Thoughts

With the Author: Your comments will be forwarded to the author when you send them to *zauthor@zondervan.com*.

With Zondervan: Submit your review of this book by writing to *zreview@zondervan.com*.

Free Online Resources at
www.zondervan.com

Zondervan AuthorTracker: Be notified whenever your favorite authors publish new books, go on tour, or post an update about what's happening in their lives at www.zondervan.com/authortracker.

Daily Bible Verses and Devotions: Enrich your life with daily Bible verses or devotions that help you start every morning focused on God. Visit www.zondervan.com/newsletters.

Free Email Publications: Sign up for newsletters on Christian living, academic resources, church ministry, fiction, children's resources, and more. Visit www.zondervan.com/newsletters.

Zondervan Bible Search: Find and compare Bible passages in a variety of translations at www.zondervanbiblesearch.com.

Other Benefits: Register yourself to receive online benefits like coupons and special offers, or to participate in research.

■ ZONDERVAN®

ZONDERVAN.com/
AUTHORTRACKER
follow your favorite authors